Praying the
Commands of Christ
into Your Life

Encountering

Jesus

Norval Hadley

With Dave and Kim Butts

"Do not think that I have come to abolish the Law or the Prophets; I have not come to abolish them but to fulfill them. I tell you the truth, until heaven and earth disappear, not the smallest letter, not the least stroke of a pen, will by any means disappear from the Law until everything is accomplished. Anyone who breaks one of the least of these commandments and teaches others to do the same will be called least in the kingdom of heaven, but whoever practices and teaches these commands will be called great in the kingdom of heaven" (Matthew 5:17–19).

—Jesus Christ

PRAYERSHOP
PUBLISHING

Terre Haute, Indiana

Prayer Shop Publishing is the publishing arm of Harvest Prayer Ministries and the Church Prayer Leaders Network. Harvest Prayer Ministries exists to transform lives through teaching prayer.

Its online prayer store, www.prayershop.org, has more than 500 prayer resources available for purchase.

ISBN: 978-1-935012-43-6

1 2 3 4 5 6 7 | 2017 2016 2015 2014 2013

Acknowledgments

I acknowledge the help of my wife, Mary, who was valuable to me in many ways in the course of preparing this manuscript. She can now enjoy the fruit of her lifelong faithfulness with Jesus Christ face-to-face, as she has gone to be with Him. Also, I wish to thank my Sunday school class at Arcadia Friends Church in California, which contributed many ideas as we experimented in the teaching of the commandments of Christ.

Special thanks to Dave Butts, chairman of the National Prayer Committee, and his wife, Kim, both authors in their own right, who spent considerable time working with me on this project. They helped shape the format to enhance the prominence of prayer in the book. Because of their contributions, we are not just reading about the commands of Christ but are praying the commands into our lives and meditating on how we can best obey them.

Table of Contents

How to Use This Book Effectively

Praying and obeying the commands of Christ is a life-changing endeavor. The commands of Jesus are balanced, affecting every area of life. As this book came together, quite apart from human effort, the Holy Spirit grouped the commands into three specific areas of impact. There are commands relating to God, relating to others, and relating to self. Obviously, there will be some overlap; however, I have categorized them by their primary area of focus and thus into three sections.

Here are my recommendations for using this book personally or corporately.

Daily: Praying through these commands each day will give you a powerful overview of the desire Jesus has for His people to obey Him and to live out holy lives before God. Consider praying through this book each month for several months or even an entire year. That will give you an opportunity to learn how to practice obedience instead of simply studying the commands devotionally.

Weekly: Take your time, and go through one command a week. Practice obedience as you ask God to teach you.

Small Group: Engage your small group or invite others to journey through these commands with you. We have included additional teachings/commands to use on our free download page at www.harvestprayer.com/resources/free-downloads.

Family: What an amazing way to teach your children to obey God! Take them through one command at a time, spending time in prayer and active obedience together.

Preface

Perhaps the most common thing we hear about the commands of Jesus is that we should "keep" them! In our culture today, many consider them just another set of rules to follow, if they even attend to the Lord at all. Following Christ is not an easy lifestyle, which is why He tells us to "enter through the narrow gate. For wide is the gate and broad is the road that leads to destruction, and many enter through it. But small is the gate and narrow the road that leads to life, and only a few find it" (Matthew 7:13–14).

How then, does the ordinary believer lean into the extraordinary to impact the kingdom through humility and obedience? I firmly believe that it is within the communion of prayer with our Father and in unified community with the Body of Christ that such abundant life is possible.

Becoming a Disciple as the Prerequisite for Making Disciples

Most believers do not equate obedience to Jesus' commands with prayer; however, it is only possible to fully obey while staying attached to the Vine through seeking His face. In our own strength it is impossible, but with the power of God unleashed through our humble asking, we can overcome the sin that entangles and step-by-step become obedient disciples.

It would seem that the one command about which the church has written and said the most is the one found in Matthew 28:18–20: "Then Jesus came to them and said, 'All authority in heaven

and on earth has been given to me. Therefore go and make disciples
of all nations, baptizing them in the name of the Father and of the
Son and of the Holy Spirit, and teaching them to obey everything
I have commanded you. And surely I am with you always, to the
very end of the age.'"

What is known as the Great Commission of Christ to His disciples is one of the last things He said to us before He left the world
to be at the right hand of the Father. Therefore, many feel this is
the command that He considered most important. The church has
given a great deal of attention to this commission to go and make
disciples of all nations; however, it seems to me that we have been
weak in our obedience to the last part of this command—"teaching
them to obey everything I have commanded you."

We have gone out with great zeal preaching the gospel and
have evangelized people of many nations, but too often we find that
those to whom we have introduced Christ later fall away. The seed
has not grown and developed so that it could bear fruit. Perhaps
part of the reason is that we have not followed up the preaching of
the good news that Jesus saves with the teaching of the things He
commanded.

Prayer as the Strategy for Evangelism and Discipleship

Prayer is now widely considered by most missiologists and missions
organizations to be the foundational strategy for carrying out and
completing the Great Commission. If prayer is the key to fulfilling
this command, then would it not be reasonable to suggest that prayer
is the primary vehicle for obeying "all that I have commanded you"?

For this devotional, I have taken a thirty-day sampling from
writing I have done on all of the commands of Jesus found in the

Gospels. These are not necessarily the most important, as they are all important; however, my prayer is that you will take them to heart and prayerfully consider how to implement them more fully into your life.

The Lord intends for us to obey His Word, not pick and choose what we wish to follow. He has our transformation in mind, not a legalistic set of rules to make our lives difficult. Yet, keeping many of these commands is certainly challenging. I suggest that after thirty days, you continue to work your way prayerfully through the additional commands found in the free download section at harvestprayer.com. I can guarantee that if you will begin to pray faithfully and then obey these commands, your life will be significantly different. You will begin to notice that, day by day, you are being transformed more fully into the image of Jesus Christ.

Wherever the followers of Jesus go to make disciples and to baptize in the name of the Father and the Son and the Holy Spirit, we should fervently be teaching them to obey all He has commanded us. By thus obeying Jesus, I believe the church will do a much stronger and more lasting work in the lives of those it influences. It is my hope that by learning to pray through the commands of Jesus using this book, you will be able to do just that, for our obedience to this command comes with a promise: "And surely I am with you always, to the very end of the age."

My Prayer

Heavenly Father, we are studying and praying through the commands of Christ out of a desire to be obedient to the Great Commission. I pray You will use this study in my life and the lives of many to make us more effective disciples of Christ and to show us how to disciple the nations that are Your inheritance (Psalm 2:8)!

Section One

God: Upward Obedience

This first section of praying the commands of Christ deals with how we relate to God. It is appropriate that we begin with our interaction with God Himself, as all of life comes from Him and is ultimately about Him. Nothing else in life will be right until we line ourselves up in right relationship with our Creator.

It is also fitting that we begin here because we are able to hear these commands straight from the mouth of the Son of God. All other spiritual teachers must rely upon secondhand resources to teach us how to relate to God. Even the biblical prophets heard from God and then passed what they heard to us. But this is God Himself speaking directly to us, telling us how to interact and live in a way that pleases Him.

Chapter 1

Love the Lord Your God

One of them, an expert in the law, tested him with this question: "Teacher, which is the greatest commandment in the Law?" Jesus replied: "'Love the Lord your God with all your heart and with all your soul and with all your mind.' This is the first and greatest commandment. And the second is like it: 'Love your neighbor as yourself.' All the Law and the Prophets hang on these two commandments." (MATTHEW 22:35—40)

Because the obeying of every other command hinges on it, I think this is the best place for us to begin. Jesus points us to our relationship with God first, and with others second. However, the two cannot be separated as they are bound together in the central command of each, which is love. Also, Jesus refers to these two commands as the greatest; therefore, we must give them special emphasis in our own hearts and lives as the foundational commands of Christ. If we are to be obedient in discipling the nations, these two commands are inextricably linked. (You will find the "second" command more completely developed and discussed at the beginning of section 2.)

Jesus, in response to the "expert in the law," indicated that this double command is basically a summary of the teaching in the first five books of the Bible—the law given through Moses and the teaching of the prophetic writers of the Old Testament. The second "greatest commandment" cannot be successfully accomplished until the first is embraced, understood, honored, and obeyed, which is why we are addressing the upwardly focused commands first in our journey through the next thirty days together. Unless believers fully grasp how to love God and worship Him in His holiness, no other commandments can be purely obeyed.

The Pharisees accepted the written Word as inspired by God; however, they also gave equal authority to oral tradition, with which Jesus was in constant conflict. They let their relationship with God be reduced to a legalistic list of rules and regulations. When God becomes only about rules, intimacy and understanding of the fullness of our relationship with Him as Father is lost in ritual. The command to love God is the most often repeated in Scripture because of the great love God has for His people, a love so intense and amazing that He gave His only Son to redeem us and give us the ultimate gift of eternal life (John 3:16).

The Message states, Jesus said, "'Love the Lord your God with all your passion and prayer and intelligence.' This is the most important, the first on any list." King David gives us perhaps the best example of one who absolutely and without question loved the Lord his God with all of his heart, soul, and mind. Dressed ceremonially for worship in a white linen ephod, David "danced before the LORD with all his might, while he and the entire house of Israel were bringing up the ark of the LORD with shouts and the sound of trumpets" (2 Samuel 6:14–15). David loved God intensely and creatively! The Psalms also testify to the depth of his desire for the Lord. He prayed earnestly, sang, played instruments, wrote music, danced—and gave honor to God with every gift, talent, and opportunity. One has only to read Psalm 63:1–8 to see the depth of longing David had for the Father.

Jesus commanded us to love the Lord our God, and Scripture punctuates this over and over again. It has been my experience that when Scripture is repetitive, we need to pay special attention and be especially focused on obedience. Take some time to read and pray through Deuteronomy 6:5; 10:12; 11:1; 11:13; 11:22; 30:16; Joshua 22:5; 1 Corinthians 8:3; and 1 John 5:3.

The Bible, especially in 1 John, talks about perfect love. If you love God with all your heart, soul, mind, and strength, then there is no room for anything that is contrary to love. Such love, John says, casts out fear (see 1 John 4:18). Perfect love is possible in this life when the Spirit has filled us and our heart has been purified by faith.

Some think loving like this is possible only after we get to heaven. But John says this love is perfected in us and gives us boldness in the day of judgment: "This is how love is made complete among us so that we will have confidence on the day of judgment: In this world we are like Jesus" (1 John 4:17).

Evelyn Christensen passed away in 2011 at the age of eighty-nine. Her life exemplified the greatest commands of Jesus, for she loved Him deeply and completely. Evelyn was best known for writing books such as *What Happens When Women Pray?*, *Lord Change Me*, and *Praying God's Way*. Yet she was perhaps most excited about her *Study Guide for Evangelism Praying*, because Evelyn had a passion and a deep sense of urgency for all people to know Christ and to be transferred from the kingdom of darkness to the eternal kingdom of her beloved King Jesus. She could barely speak a sentence without the name of Jesus in it. Her last words were "It's beautiful! It's beautiful! It's beautiful! Jesus is holding my hand." Evelyn loved Jesus with all of her heart, soul, and mind. And she loved others so intensely that she couldn't bear the thought of anyone dying without His love embedded in their hearts.

Here is a powerful thought: If everyone loved and obeyed the two greatest commandments as Evelyn did, there would be no need for the law. How would you like to live in a world like that? I think we will in our next life when Jesus is ruler over all.

Connect with Christ

Prayerfully ask Jesus this question: "Lord, how am I doing with this command?" Allow the Holy Spirit to speak to your heart as you wait before Him with integrity and humility. Take some time (as long as you need) to quiet your spirit and wait before God as you allow this command to sink more deeply into your life.

Jesus, as I sit here in silence before You, please give me a more complete picture about what loving God with all of my heart, soul, and mind really means for my life. Speak to my heart so that I will know what You desire for me to do to embrace this command more completely and so that Your Holy Spirit can transform me more fully into Your image.

Consider the Command

1. What do you think about the author's assertion that "perfect love is possible in this life when the Spirit has filled us

and our heart has been purified by faith"?

2. How does this kind of love fulfill the law (Romans 13:10)?

3. All of us know people who are good, moral, just, and who do kind things for others but who have no relationship with Jesus. Some don't even believe in the existence of God. Where does this come from apart from knowing Him? Are their actions for God's sake or for their own? Take some time to think through and discuss this question, as it applies to many people you know.

Praying It into Practice

1. Ask the Lord to teach you what it means to love Him with all your heart, soul, mind, and strength.

2. Go to Psalm 145 and read to the Lord what His own Word says about Him. Pray these words back to God as an expression of love to Him.

My Prayer

Lord, You know that I love You. Help me to love You more. With everything that is in me, I want to love You with the perfect love that casts out all fear. I thank You that according to Your Word, the Holy Spirit has poured Your love into me. I receive that by faith, with gratitude. Help me to allow Your amazing love to flow through me into others. I know that You don't love me because I am so lovable but in spite of my unloveliness. Help me to love like that!

Chapter 2

Do Not Live by Bread Alone

Jesus answered, "It is written: 'Man shall not live on bread alone,
but on every word that comes from the mouth of God.'" (MATTHEW 4:4)

Mike Bickle, in his book *Passion for Jesus,* wrote: "Jesus had no sin, wrong thinking or impure motives that gave Satan legal access to His life. Satan could find nothing in Jesus—not one inch of territory—to which he could lay claim and thus gain access to Jesus' heart. The enemy continually seeks occasions where he can obtain a legal entry point into our lives. Just as Jesus resisted and conquered Satan's effort to tempt him by using the Word of God, so we must use the scripture like a sword to defeat Satan's effort to gain entry into our lives" (p. 85).

In Scripture, the first command uttered by Christ is "Man shall not live on bread alone, but on every word that comes from the mouth of God" (Matthew 4:4).

This is one of several commands which Jesus spoke to a certain person at a certain time and place. It could be argued that these commands were not intended to be followed by all of us. Nevertheless, usually we will find something of value for each of us as we study them. This particular command was spoken by Jesus to the devil. Jesus had been taken into the wilderness by the Spirit of God for forty days and nights, and there was tempted by the devil. The Bible says, "After fasting forty days and forty nights, he was hungry" (Matthew 4:2).

Employing a device he uses with all of us, Satan saw a potential moment of weakness and sought to destroy Jesus at that very point. He urged Jesus to turn the stones into bread—to perform a spectacular miracle to satisfy his own physical need, which was contrary to the will of God. It was at this crucial juncture that Jesus refused the devil and resisted him by quoting, "Man does not live on bread alone, but on every word that comes from the mouth of God." Jesus is indicating the importance of the spiritual versus the physical as the support of the very essence of life.

The important lesson for us is that we can resist the devil, just as Jesus did, by using the "sword of the Spirit, which is the Word of God" (Ephesians 6:17). In fact, we can live by every word that proceeds from the mouth of God. At that time and in that situation, the meaning of Jesus' words was, "I am not going to yield to your will. I am going to continue to do the will of God no matter how hungry I get." There are many instances in the Bible when the devil is battled using the Word of God such as Psalm 119:11: "I have hidden your word in my heart that I might not sin against you."

I met the girl who became my wife during the first week of our first year together at a Christian college, George Fox University. We were in a get-acquainted mixer and the director asked us to pick a partner. I looked around the circle and found the prettiest girl there and said, "Don't go away." And she never did until she died after sixty-one years of marriage.

For me, that college experience was like a week at a Christian camp where relationships bloom. We decided to wait to get married until we graduated and I could earn enough to support a family. That turned into four long years. We also decided that we wanted to save physical intimacy until after marriage, so that meant resisting a lot of temptation. The verse that sustained me was 1 Corinthians 10:13: "No temptation has overtaken you except what is common to mankind. And God is faithful; he will not let you be tempted beyond what you can bear. But when you are tempted, he will also provide a way out so that you can endure it." So I prayed in faith that God would always provide the way out, and He answered my prayer. He was faithful to me as I yielded to His command to live not by bread alone, but by His Word and example.

Connect with Christ

Prayerfully ask Jesus this question: "Lord, how am I doing with this command?" Allow the Holy Spirit to speak to your heart as you wait before Him with integrity and humility. Take some time (as long as you need) to quiet your spirit and wait before God. Allow this command to sink more deeply into your life.

Jesus, as I sit here in silence before You, please give me a more complete picture about what it means to live by every word that comes from the mouth of God. Speak to my heart so that I will know what I should do to embrace this command more completely. May Your Holy Spirit transform me more fully into Your image.

Consider the Command

1. How do you feel about applying the command that Jesus spoke to the devil to your own life? Is this a valid command for us today? Why or why not?

2. Why do you believe it would have been wrong for Jesus to turn stones into bread?

3. Do you believe that you are equipped to resist the devil, using the Word of God as Jesus did? What can you do to be better equipped?

Praying It into Practice

1. Carefully examine your prayer life for one week. How many of your requests are for your own needs? Would you say that you are out of balance, praying more from your own heart than from the heart of God? On what do the majority of your prayers focus?

2. Ask the Lord to help you use His Word to resist the devil. Along with that prayer, make it a practice to bring the Word of God into your prayers daily. This will help you align your prayers with God's desires instead of just your own.

My Prayer

Father, I thank You that You provide everything I need for this life as well as for eternity. Your Word tells me to ask for daily bread, the provision that I need. But I'm also grateful that You have given me Your eternal Word to feed upon. Fill me with Your Word that I might overflow with the life of Your Spirit. Show me how to use Your Word as Jesus did to resist the devil. I submit to Your Word, Father, that the devil might flee from me.

Chapter 3

Follow Me

"Come, follow me," Jesus said, "and I will send you out to fish for people." (MARK 1:17)

A fter the temptations in the wilderness, Jesus entered His public ministry. Almost immediately He began gathering disciples. Matthew's account says that Jesus was walking by the Sea of Galilee and saw two fishermen who were brothers: Simon, called Peter, and Andrew. He said to them, "Follow me, and I will make you fishers of men" (4:19, KJV). Then Jesus saw James and John, the fishermen sons of Zebedee. The Bible says that without hesitation all four left their nets and followed Jesus. This was a big decision for them. Following Jesus required two of them to leave their father, who was probably up in years. All of them had to abandon their boats, their hired servants, and their livelihoods.

The next day, as Jesus headed toward Galilee, He had an encounter with Philip and called him to "follow me" (John 1:43). Philip not only followed Jesus, but he believed in Him so thoroughly that he went immediately and found Nathaniel, telling him, "We have found the one Moses wrote about in the Law, and about whom the prophets also wrote—Jesus of Nazareth, the son of Joseph" (John 1:45). Phillip was so convinced that he made a complete commitment to Christ at their first meeting.

What did Jesus mean when He said, "Follow me"? Did He mean, "Come with Me; I want to show you something?" Or did He mean, "Follow Me for the rest of your life?" Clearly, we believe it was the latter. The obedience of these disciples is a beautiful example for us to follow. We can either obey and follow Him, enjoying the peace, assurance, and adventure He gives, or we can decide to go our own way, losing all the benefits afforded only to Jesus' disciples. True to His promise, the first disciples did indeed have the thrill of catching men.

The "follow me" command was issued again in Matthew 9:9 to Matthew (also called Levi), who left everything, including a very lucrative business, to follow Jesus. But before he did, Levi invited all his friends, including many other tax collectors, to a great feast. I'm sure the reason for the feast was to give them a chance to learn of the change that had come into his life and to meet his new Master.

This is a great idea. Why shouldn't new converts have Levi dinners today? It always helps a person make a clean break from the old lifestyle when that person gives a clear testimony to old friends. Those who are worth keeping as friends will join in following Christ, or at least stay close enough to hear more. Those who are not will drop the new convert like a hot potato, and the convert will be better off for it.

The decision to follow Jesus has meant everything to me. I've traveled for Him in seventy-five countries, been shot at a couple of times, and have faced several situations when I didn't know whether I would live or die. Because I had committed my life into His hands, I didn't have to wonder whether He would give me His best. When trouble has come, I have been able to handle it with His help because I have answered the call to follow Him wherever He leads. What a blessed assurance!

Connect with Christ

Prayerfully ask Jesus this question: "Lord, how am I doing with this command?" Allow the Holy Spirit to speak to your heart as you wait before Him with integrity and humility. Take some time (as long as you need) to quiet your spirit and wait before God as you allow this command to sink more deeply into your life.

Jesus, as I sit here in silence before You, please give me a more complete picture about what following You really means for my life. Speak to my heart so that I will know what You desire for me to do to embrace this command more completely and so that Your Holy Spirit can transform me more fully into Your image.

Consider the Command

1. What does it mean to you to follow Jesus? What has it cost you to be His follower? Has the cost been worth it? Why or why not? If you are not following Him as fully as you would like, or once did, what do you think it means to "count the cost" in order to be His disciple?

2. Do you believe there is adequate challenge in the church today to really follow Jesus? What can be done to help people understand the reality of following Him?

3. What has been the hardest thing Jesus has ever asked you to do as His follower?

4. What do you think of the author's idea for those who have recently accepted Jesus to have a Levi dinner? Would that be difficult for you? Why or why not?

Praying It into Practice

1. If you have never clearly spoken these words to Jesus, "Lord, I will follow You," then pray that now.

2. Make a list for yourself of what you believe would change in your life physically and spiritually over the next month if you heard Jesus say to you, "Come, follow Me." Present the list to the Lord in prayer.

My Prayer

Lord Jesus, You have indeed said, "Come, follow me" to all whom You have called. Help me to take that seriously. No hesitation, no pulling back, no disobedience. Lord, I will follow You wherever You lead, whatever it costs. I can't do that in my own strength. Even to follow You, I need You! May Your grace so work within me that it encourages other believers to follow You with all that is in them.

Chapter 4

Lay Up Treasures in Heaven

Do not store up for yourselves treasures on earth, where moths and vermin destroy, and where thieves break in and steal. But store up for yourselves treasures in heaven, where moths and vermin do not destroy, and where thieves do not break in and steal. For where your treasure is, there your heart will be also. (MATTHEW 6:19–21)

In Matthew 6:19, Jesus not only tells us what we should obey, but also what we should *not* do: "Do not store up for yourselves treasures on earth. . . . But store up for yourselves treasures in heaven." Earthly treasures can be destroyed, consumed, or stolen; however, heavenly rewards cannot. Where we store the things we treasure will show the Father what we value, because our hearts will be tied to either earth or heaven.

Building material wealth in this life is relatively unimportant compared to laying up treasures in heaven. Jesus is giving us the kingdom. He is giving us eternal life, the hope of heaven. What we have now is a temporary thing. What we will have for all eternity is the important thing.

It seems significant that when we lay up treasures in heaven it is for ourselves. What we invest in eternal values will be returned to us personally. The point Jesus is making is that worldly treasures are corruptible. They deteriorate. Thieves steal them. Treasures laid up in heaven have a security that remains, like nothing on earth.

How do we lay up treasure in heaven? Giving to advance the work of the kingdom of God is one obvious way. Working to build godly character is another, developing minds that can enjoy great thoughts of God and hearts that transcend selfishness by doing loving acts of service. Such treasures have eternal value, and will abide forever.

There is clearly much reward that comes from obeying this command. It has been the experience of many Christians that you don't have to wait for heaven to enjoy some of the blessings of laying up treasures there. God begins to reward in this life the faithful steward of resources. When He said, "Where your treasure is, there your heart will be also," He is saying that when you are laying up treasures on earth, there is little affection left for heavenly riches. All of us know executives, entertainers, or even people just like us who have given their whole lives to acquiring material wealth only to find that the rewards were not satisfying. They ended life destitute of things of real value—treasures in heaven. Conversely, when with all one's heart a person prepares for eternity, that person not only receives eternal reward, but also material things here fall into proper perspective.

I have a missionary friend who is a gifted athlete and coach. I'm not sure how much money he could have made if he had stayed in the United States and coached, but he chose to be a missionary in southern Ireland. He uses athletics to win people to the Lord there through basketball camps and sports training. He's written a tract, *Meet My Head Coach,* which has now been translated into several languages. He has also planted two churches in a land that is just a little more than one percent evangelical Christian. My friend might have become wealthy pursuing his skills in the United States, but he chose to lay up treasure in heaven, and that treasure will surely be considerable.

Connect with Christ

Prayerfully ask Jesus this question: "Lord, how am I doing with this command?" Allow the Holy Spirit to speak to your heart as you wait before Him with integrity and humility. Take some time (as long as you need) to quiet your spirit and wait before God. Allow this command to sink more deeply into your life.

Jesus, as I sit here in silence before You, please give me a more complete picture about what laying up treasure in heaven really means for my life. Speak to my heart so that I will know what You desire for me to do to embrace this command more completely and so that Your Holy Spirit can transform me more fully into Your image.

Consider the Command

1. Consider the amount of time you have spent accumulating worldly treasures: working, investing, saving, creating, and perhaps many more ways. Now think about the amount of time you have spent accumulating heavenly treasures. How does this comparison make you feel?

2. What sort of actions do you believe store up treasures in heaven?

3. Have you thought about heavenly rewards? What do you believe the Lord is referring to?

Praying It into Practice

1. Ask the Lord to show you your heavenly bank account balance. Have you been adequately preparing for heaven?
2. Pray about your heart condition regarding where your treasure is. Heart surgery may be required by the Lord.

My Prayer

Father, forgive me for being far too focused on accumulating wealth here in this life. Give me heaven's perspective on what is important. Cleanse my heart of wanting more and more of that which will not last, while ignoring that which is imperishable. Give me a giving heart. Let me hold loosely to the things of this world. Show me how to lay up ever-increasing treasure in heaven.

Chapter 5

Give Generously

Give, and it will be given to you. A good measure, pressed down, shaken together and running over, will be poured into your lap. For with the measure you use, it will be measured to you. (LUKE 6:38)

What a great statement of God's faithfulness and generosity! If you give a thimbleful to the needy and to God, you will get back a thimbleful of blessing. If you give a tubful you will get back a tubful of blessing and reward. This is an excellent commentary on the old saying, "You cannot outgive God."

I've used Luke 6:38 to encourage giving money to support missions and the work of the kingdom, and I think it can be rightly applied for such use. But the *John Phillips Commentary* cites the context to show that Jesus is speaking here primarily of relationships with others. Give love and you will get love. Give understanding and you will get understanding. Show compassion and others will be compassionate toward you. Give yourself, don't condemn, don't judge, show concern, be generous, and you will be richly rewarded.

Second Corinthians 9:6 says the same thing. "Remember this: Whoever sows sparingly will also reap sparingly, and whoever sows generously will also reap generously." Here the context has to do with giving funds.

This command is similar to Jesus' teaching that states, "For whoever wants to save his life will lose it, but whoever loses his life for me will find it" (Matthew 16:25). It is in giving that we gain. Jim Elliot, a missionary who was martyred at the hands of the Auca Indians, said, "He is no fool who gives what he cannot keep to gain what he cannot lose."

My wife and I first heard about faith promise giving in 1950 when the famous mission-minded pastor, Oswald Smith, from Toronto, Canada, made a presentation at the Youth for Christ convention at Winona Lake, Indiana. We were deeply moved, and by faith, promised to give a second tithe. We were earning about $200 a month then, which wasn't much even in those days, and we got that only through the offerings at meetings where the men's quartet I participated in sang. God so honored our faith that we have never doubted His willingness to keep the promise of this command from that day on. We received back much more that year in added income than we gave, and God has been faithful every year since.

God may not always give back more in money than we give to Him, for God looks at the heart of our intentions. Giving to get more wealth is not the best motive, so we must continually examine our hearts to be sure that our objectives are pure. We give because we love Him and want to obey Him and help in the world-wide mission of His church. Often, His faithful ones have seen this promise fulfilled literally with material reward. And always, there are spiritual and relational rewards. Our giving, whether of funds, time, or talent, should always bring honor and glory to God and the purposes of His kingdom alone.

Connect with Christ

Prayerfully ask Jesus this question: "Lord, how am I doing with this command?" Allow the Holy Spirit to speak to your heart as you wait before Him with integrity and humility. Take some time (as long as you need) to quiet your spirit and wait before God, allowing this command to sink more deeply into your life.

Jesus, as I sit here in silence before You, please give me a more complete picture about what giving generously really means for my life. Speak to my heart so that I will know what You desire for me to do to embrace this command more completely, and so that Your Holy Spirit can transform me more fully into Your image.

Consider the Command

1. Do you have the faith to believe God's promise to you as you obey this command? Why or why not?

2. How have you seen this verse work in your life financially? Be specific. Have you seen how God stepped in to outgive you in a specific situation?

Praying It into Practice

1. Ask the Lord if there is an area of giving in which you have not been obedient. Determine to obey whatever He shows you.

2. Thank the Lord for His generosity to you. Ask Him to show you ways to reflect that generosity to others to bring Him honor.

My Prayer

Father, You are the Giver of every good and perfect gift. All that we have comes from You. You are our faithful provider. Thank You! Help me to reflect Your giving nature in my life. Not only, Lord, in the giving of finances, but in my time, my love, my concern for others. Teach me to trust You as I pour out what You have given me with the generosity that I see in who You are.

Chapter 6

Be Restfully Busy

Come to me, all you who are weary and burdened, and I will give you rest. Take my yoke upon you and learn from me, for I am gentle and humble in heart, and you will find rest for your souls. For my yoke is easy and my burden is light. (MATTHEW 11:28–30)

In Matthew 11:27, Jesus is praying. In that prayer, He speaks more clearly than in almost any other passage of His relationship to God the Father as His Son. He speaks of His unique role in revealing the Father to people. Then He says "Come to me, all you who are weary and burdened, and I will give you rest." Here is a wonderful command and promise to those who are tired in soul and restless. There is a blessed quietness available for your soul. The One who reveals the Father to us wants to give us a rest, best described in Hebrews 4 as a rest like God's rest on the seventh day *4:9/0* of creation, a Sabbath rest for the people of God, wherein we cease from our labors.

While Jesus wants to cause you to rest, He speaks of a yoke. A yoke was the important part of a harness worn by work animals. Can He be speaking of rest and work at the same time?

I think so. There is no absolute freedom from every yoke. Those who want to be completely free often find themselves under an oppressive yoke—of drugs or materialism, of various kinds of poverty, of various desires they cannot control. That yoke becomes a bondage, and those under it find they are not free. Jesus promises, by contrast, that His yoke is easy and His burden is light. He is saying, "Yoke yourself with Me because My task for you is shared and easy and My burden is light."

I traveled some with a Swiss missionary to Indonesia on furlough who used to pray for his colleagues back on the mission field, "Lord, keep them restfully busy." I think my friend knew that the pressure of the work, maybe increased because of his absence, could lead to stress. Therefore, he was praying that his colleagues would do their work with the blessing and help of the Lord to such an extent that work would go well and, in fact, even be restful instead of a burden.

Some have supposed that at Jesus' carpenter shop, they made the best yokes in all of Galilee. Maybe there was a sign on the outside that said, "My yokes fit well." This is certainly true of the spiritual yoke He gives to all who follow Him, or as the term "yoke" implies, who work alongside Him in His task. There is an implied warning that if we do not come to Him, we will not find rest; we will be tired, and we will experience an oppressive yoke and carry a heavy burden.

I heard one preacher say, "Suppose I brought before you two people, one who had served God with love and devotion all his life, and the other who had served Satan all his life. You could just look into their faces and know which one has the hardest task master." So many of God's people have an independent spirit, which keeps them from experiencing the lightness of depending upon the loving Father, who desires to carry our burdens. When we do not obey His command to yield them up to His care, we will most certainly experience the consequences of our rebellion. Yet, if we will take Him at His word and obey Him, Jesus' yoke is easy and His burden is light.

Connect with Christ

Prayerfully ask Jesus this question: "Lord, how am I doing with this command?" Allow the Holy Spirit to speak to your heart as you wait before Him with integrity and humility. Take some time (as long as you need) to quiet your spirit and wait before God. Allow this command to sink more deeply into your life.

Jesus, as I sit here in silence before You, please give me a more complete picture about what taking on Your yoke really means for my life. Speak to my heart so that I will know what You desire for me to do to embrace this command more completely and so that Your Holy Spirit can transform me more fully into Your image.

Consider the Command

1. Have you ever been tired as you served the Lord? Do you think this verse says we will never be tired? Why or why not? *We will get physically tired but find rest in His promise.*

2. How have you reconciled the biblical commands to work and to rest in your life?

3. What does the yoke of the Lord mean to you as you deal with this direct command of Jesus? *The assurance that He shares the burden and lightens the load.*

Praying It into Practice

1. As you pray, picture the Lord placing His yoke upon you. Do you feel burdened now, or is there a sense of peace and rest?

2. Confess to the Lord the times you have tried to do His work in your own strength, wearing yourself out in the process. Thank Him for His yoke and ask Him to show you how to find rest for your soul.

My Prayer

Lord Jesus, as I consider this command of Yours to take up Your yoke, I am reminded of Psalm 23 and what it means to follow a shepherd who knows where there is water, provision, and protection. Thank You for Your yoke. I gladly take it because I know that it means I am yoked to You. You are the One who carries the load. You are the One who knows where we are going. As I walk through this life yoked to You, You have promised to teach me Your ways. You desire that I learn gentleness and humility from You so that I might find rest for my soul. Thank You, Lord Jesus, for Your easy yoke and light burden.

Chapter 7

Take Up Your Cross

And anyone who does not carry his cross and follow me cannot be my disciple. (LUKE 14:27)

In Luke 14, Jesus is teaching on the cost of being His follower. He didn't want disciples who were only partially committed. Before He spoke the words above, He said prospective disciples should "hate" father and mother, wife and brothers and sisters and their own lives also in order to be His disciples (v. 26). That is a hard teaching. We know that Jesus wants us to love family. He often used strong language to get our attention and teach us an important truth. I've been helped when a wise teacher explained it this way: By contrast to our love for Jesus, our commitment to family looks like hate.

Jesus followed this shocking statement by saying that if one wants to build a tower he first sits down and counts the cost to be sure he has enough money to finish it (Luke 14:28). No one wants to be mocked because he can't finish what he started. Then He said, when a king goes to war he first must consider if his ten thousand troops can beat an enemy with twenty thousand. And if he decides he can't, he negotiates a peace treaty.

As director of the Evangelical Friends Mission, I've ministered to Christians, especially overseas, who had to sit down before they decided to accept Christ and consider whether they were ready to face the opposition from the enemies of the gospel, enemies that would include their own family members and community leaders. In fact, at least one of our coworkers in Nepal often told me he knew people who wanted to become Christians, but he didn't let them because they had not yet prepared to pay the price. He didn't want his converts to be mocked because they could not follow through on their decision to forsake the heathen religion of their area and accept Christ.

Jesus knew what His followers would face and He wanted us to be prepared. I understand that though we in the United States have not had to face severe persecution for our faith, the time may be coming when we will. Persecution is predicted as we come toward the last days. Jesus said in Matthew 24:21, "For then there will be great distress, unequaled from the beginning of the world until now—and never to be equaled again." In that same message, Jesus promised a great reward for those who remain faithful. He talked about the servant who remains wise and faithful in spite of persecution and says, "It will be good for that servant whose master finds him doing so when he returns. I tell you the truth, he will put him in charge of all his possessions" (Matthew 24:46–47).

Connect with Christ

Prayerfully ask Jesus this question: "Lord, how am I doing with this command?" Allow the Holy Spirit to speak to your heart as you

wait before Him with integrity and humility. Take some time (as long as you need) to quiet your spirit and wait before God. Allow this command to sink more deeply into your life.

Jesus, as I sit here in silence before You, please give me a more complete picture about what carrying my cross and following You really means for my life. Speak to my heart so that I will know what You desire for me to do to embrace this command more completely, and so that Your Holy Spirit can transform me more fully into Your image.

Consider the Command

1. What do you believe it means to take up your cross and follow Jesus? *He asks for All!*
2. Have you ever faced persecution or even ridicule for following Jesus? Recall this situation and see if it fits carrying your cross.
3. When you accepted Christ, did you count the cost? Did anyone help you think through what it would mean to follow Jesus? How can you do this for others?

Praying It into Practice

1. Pray for your brothers and sisters in Christ who are facing persecution for following Jesus.
2. If you feel compelled, tell the Lord of your willingness to take up your cross and follow Him. Ask Him for strength to face whatever opposition might come, even if it comes from your own family. If you do not feel that you can give yourself fully to the Lord in this way, ask Him to give you the courage to take this step of faith.

My Prayer

Lord, I have always been amazed by your willingness to take up Your cross on my behalf. Thank You! Because of that love, I want to take up my cross and follow You. I affirm with the apostle Paul that I have been crucified with Christ and that it is no longer I who live, but You, Lord Jesus, living out Your life in me. So, I cling to the old rugged cross today. Grant me the strength to hold to the cross, regardless of the cost.

Chapter 8

Proclaiming the Lord's Death until He Comes

While they were eating, Jesus took bread, gave thanks and broke it, and gave it to his disciples, saying, "Take and eat; this is my body." Then he took the cup, gave thanks and offered it to them, saying, "Drink from it, all of you. This is my blood of the covenant, which is poured out for many for the forgiveness of sins."
(MATTHEW 26:26—28)

This is the first institution of the Lord's Supper. It is mentioned also in Mark 14, Luke 22, and 1 Corinthians 11. Matthew and Mark say He blessed the bread. Luke says He gave thanks. Matthew Henry's commentary says Jesus was not blessing the bread, but giving thanks to God who gives us bread and wine. This could also be considered a precedent for giving thanks before a meal.

It is significant that in Bible times they did not cut the bread, but broke it. Bread then was thin and brittle. Since the bread represented the body of Jesus, which was broken for us, it is appropriate that it be broken in this sacrament. As our life depends on the bread God provides, so our eternal life depends on Christ's body, which was broken for us.

The cup represents the blood of Jesus, which was shed for the remission of sins. Jesus said it is "my blood of the new covenant." It is the new offering of God's only Son that ushered in the means of salvation that we are commemorating. In 1 Corinthians 11, Paul issues a stern warning that one who eats the bread and drinks the cup in an unworthy manner will be guilty of the body and blood of the Lord and will bring judgment upon himself. Since the blood is for the remission of sins, Paul is saying that if we partake while sinning we are in danger of judgment.

The Jews had a similar sacrament known as the Seder, the traditional Passover week dinner celebrated by the Hebrews since the Exodus. This meal is a thanksgiving celebration, commemorating God's protection, deliverance, and redemption. It was at this meal, the seder, that Jesus instituted Holy Communion, the Lord's Supper. He was observing with His disciples the ritual meal to commemorate Israel's redemption from slavery in Egypt according to Exodus 12:14–20. They ate unleavened bread according to the Scriptures. The cup of the fruit of the vine was a traditional part of the ritual meal. Jesus' reference was to the elements of the ritual meal with application to his own sacrifice as the "lamb" and to inaugurate the new covenant prophesied in Jeremiah 31:31–34. "'This is the covenant I will make with the house of Israel after that time,' declares the LORD. 'I will put my law in their minds and write it on their hearts. I will be their God, and they will be my people'" (v. 33).

According to Paul, Jesus told His disciples, "Do this, whenever you drink it, in remembrance of me" and told them that when they observe Communion they are proclaiming the Lord's death till He comes. (see 1 Corinthians 11:25–26). Thus, as His disciples today, partaking of the sacrament should be a time of remembering the Lord's death and thanking Him for His great sacrifice so we can be saved from the penalty for sin.

Connect with Christ

Prayerfully ask Jesus this question: "Lord, how am I doing with this command?" Allow the Holy Spirit to speak to your heart as you wait before Him with integrity and humility. Take some time (as long as you need) to quiet your spirit and wait before God. Allow this command to sink more deeply into your life.

Jesus, as I sit here in silence before You, please give me a more complete picture about what remembering You through the sacrament of the Lord's Supper really means for my life. Speak to my heart so that I will know what You desire for me to do to embrace this command more completely and so that Your Holy Spirit can transform me more fully into Your image.

Consider the Command

1. What do you think about as you prepare to partake of the Lord's Supper? *His death on the cross*

2. Have you considered the idea that as our bodies depend upon the physical bread (food), so our eternal life is dependent on Christ's body, broken for us? How might that change the way you observe Communion?

3. Have there been times when you have chosen not to partake of Communion? If so, what was the reason? *Yes, once, the Lord spoke to me about something I needed to make right.*

Praying It into Practice

1. An ancient term for Communion is the Eucharist, which means to give thanks. Give thanks to the Lord for providing for you the meal of Remembrance.
2. Though the Lord's Supper is normally done with others, there are many who partake as a personal time of worship. If you are comfortable doing this, prepare the elements as well as your heart and use today's devotional to lead you into a time of prayer and the Lord's Supper.

My Prayer

What a feast You have prepared for us, Lord! Your own body and Your own blood, the sacrifice of God's own Lamb who takes away the sins of the world. Thank You for Your sacrifice. Thank You for giving us this feast of remembrance. As I consider the bread and the wine, I realize that without Your death, I would not have life. I bow in worship and adoration before You this day. Thank You for this amazing new covenant that brings me into right relationship with You because of what You have done on the cross.

Chapter 9

Remain in Me

Remain in me, and I will remain in you. No branch can bear
fruit by itself; it must remain in the vine. Neither can you bear
fruit unless you remain in me. (JOHN 15:4)

What do you suppose it means to remain in Jesus? The King
James Version of the Bible uses the word "abide," which
according to Dictionary.com means "to remain; continue" and "to
have one's abode." It includes the idea of sustaining, withstanding,
accepting without opposition or question, and even suffering for
and submitting to. All those ideas seem to fit a right relationship
with Christ.

Maybe the best way to understand what Jesus is asking of us
is to consider how He used the word "remain." We are to relate to
Him as a branch relates to a vine. He said, "I am the vine; you are
the branches. If a man remains in me and I in him, he will bear
much fruit; apart from me you can do nothing. If anyone does not
remain in me, he is like a branch that is thrown away and withers;

such branches are picked up, thrown into the fire and burned. If you remain in me and my words remain in you, ask whatever you wish, and it will be given you. This is to my Father's glory, that you bear much fruit, showing yourselves to be my disciples" (John 15:5–8).

This means that abiding in Christ, maintaining a life-giving connection to Him like a branch to a vine, is absolutely essential if we are to be productive Christians. Christ offers to live in us and invites us to live in Him, make our abode in Him, and remain there, accept Him without question, submit to Him, and be willing to suffer for Him. Abiding not only enables us to bear fruit, but if His word also abides in us we can ask what we want and it shall be done for us. What a generous promise and benefit, a promise He repeats in John 16:24: "Until now you have not asked for anything in my name. Ask and you will receive, and your joy will be complete."

Jesus speaks more fully about His intent as we remain in Him: "As the Father has loved me, so have I loved you. Now remain in my love. If you obey my commands, you will remain in my love, just as I have obeyed my Father's commands and remain in his love. I have told you this so that my joy may be in you and that your joy may be complete" (John 15:9–11). Jesus tells us that remaining in Him also means to remain in His love. By obeying His commands, we remain within the love of Jesus, which results in the joy of Jesus being made complete in us.

One of the ministries of Evangelical Friends Mission, which I led for nine years, is in Nepal. Bob Adhikary is the leader now. He has shared many stories of new converts who choose to remain in Christ even through severe persecution. One of these individuals is Shree Ram, who grew up being mocked because he was blind. People told him that he was a curse to his family and that he was

not worthy to live. Because of this, one day, Shree Ram decided
to commit suicide. He bought a rope and tried to hang himself in
his house, but the rope broke and he fell to the ground. God had
different plans for Shree Ram. Two believers, Kumar and Rebica,
moved to Shree Ram's area and started sharing the gospel with
everyone. Shree Ram heard the gospel and was drawn by the Lord.
Because he found out, through the gospel, that God loved him and
that he was not just a throwaway and a burden to society, Shree
Ram accepted Jesus as his Savior.

Shree Ram paid a heavy price for his decision. When he became
a Christian, his parents began treating him badly. They stopped giving him food to eat; so he had to go to the jungle to gather whatever
he can find. But Shree Ram did not grow discouraged. He began
helping Kumar and Rebica in their ministry. God gifted Shree Ram
with a good singing voice, so now he sings for the Lord. Even though
he cannot see, he is able to hear and grasp the Word of God. Recently, he brought three of his friends to the Lord. Shree Ram says that
he has found rest in God, he has joy in his life, and he wants to make
his life count for the Lord by serving Him. By remaining in the love
of Jesus, Shree Ram's joy has been made complete.

As important as it is to abide in Him, it is equally devastating
to disobey this command. We are not only unproductive and inef-
fective in trying to bear fruit for Him in our own strength, but we
wither and are cast aside like a dead branch that is thrown into the
fire. If you are a Christian who is out of fellowship with Christ, I
urge you to come back to a close relationship with Him by confession and repentance. Then commune with Him daily by prayer and
Bible reading (two vital and important ways to remain in Him). He
longs to welcome you back.

Connect with Christ

Prayerfully ask Jesus this question: "Lord, how am I doing with this command?" Allow the Holy Spirit to speak to your heart as you wait before Him with integrity and humility. Take some time (as long as you need) to quiet your spirit and wait before God. Allow this command to sink more deeply into your life.

Jesus, as I sit here in silence before You, please give me a more complete picture about what remaining in You really means for my life. Speak to my heart so that I will know what You desire for me to do to embrace this command more completely and so that Your Holy Spirit can transform me more fully into Your image.

Consider the Command

1. Would you describe your own Christian experience as remaining (abiding) in Christ? Why or why not?

2. The author suggests that prayer and spending time in Scripture is essential for abiding. Are there other things you do to abide in Christ? What are they?

3. What happens to a Christian who does not remain in Christ?

Praying It into Practice

1. Affirm to the Lord in prayer that He is indeed the Vine and that you are delighted to be a branch that is attached to Him. Ask Him to help you stay firmly attached.

2. Consider the lack of effort required for a branch to produce fruit. It's all dependent upon the attachment to the vine. Sit quietly before the Lord and ask Him to show you what it means to abide in Him. Consider that spiritual

fruit may have been produced just through this simple act of prayer.

My Prayer

Lord, how encouraging it is to hear Your words of invitation to abide in You. I accept! With all my heart, I long to abide in You, to dwell always with You and in You. Thank You for the picture of the Vine and the branch. Through Your precious Spirit, I choose to stay attached and allow Your life and power to flow in me and through me. Produce fruit in me that is lasting and attributable only to Your Spirit at work.

Section Two

Others: Outward Obedience

E ven those who reject the divinity of Jesus acknowledge the astonishing example and teachings on love that marked His life. Some have tried to separate the teachings of Jesus on loving others from the person of Jesus. It's just not possible! The commands of Jesus regarding the way we treat one another are so radical that it takes the supernatural power of God at work within us to fulfill these commands.

You will notice in this section about others that Jesus repeats Himself numerous times on similar themes. When we find repetition in Scripture, it is always an indication that He wants us to be especially attentive—not just to obey the command but to recognize how obeying these commands will shape the kingdom of God for His glory to be made known.

That's why the commands of Christ are presented to you in the context of prayer. It takes more than great self-discipline to "turn the other cheek" or to love your enemies. It takes the power of God at work to do this. As you commit to obeying these commands of Jesus, make them a part of your regular daily prayer life. Ask the Lord to love others through you.

Chapter 10

And the Second Is Like It

And the second is like it: "Love your neighbor as yourself."
(MATTHEW 22:39)

So in everything, do to others what you would have them do to you,
for this sums up the Law and the Prophets. (MATTHEW 7:12)

The apostle Paul reiterates that love is the fulfilling of the law:
"The entire law is summed up in a single command: 'Love
your neighbor as yourself'" (Galatians 5:14). To treat others as you
would like to be treated is one of the best outward expressions of
inner love. If everyone would do that, there would be no need for
law. Thus, it really can be the fulfilling of the law.

Suppose someone wrongs you. The natural human response is
to try to get even—hurt him back. This is exactly what gives rise to
a great deal of crime and violence. If in response you treat that person as you would like to be treated, then no crime would occur and
there would be no need for law. Forgiveness has been and always

will be the key to treating others in Christlike ways when we have been treated badly.

There are two rules for determining the best action or reaction: (1) What would Jesus do in this situation? and (2) what would I like done to me in a similar situation? If we would always let the answers to those questions govern our actions, there would be much less pain and hurt in our world.

I was teaching about Matthew 7:12 in a church in Rwanda right after the 1994 genocide there. Between five hundred thousand and one million people lost their lives in approximately one hundred days as ethnic violence surged out of control between the Hutus and the Tutsis. As an illustration, I brought two little boys up front. Suppose boy A strikes boy B, so then boy B gets boy C and they both strike back at boy A. Then, boy A gets boy D and so forth. The fight only escalates. As I taught that each person should treat others as he or she would like to be treated, there was great understanding with much miraculous forgiveness extended. These people clearly saw how a forgiving heart overcomes a heart bent on anger and revenge. Healing took place that day.

During this same trip, one of the Rwandan pastors spoke in a conference we held for pastors from Rwanda, Burundi, Congo, and Kenya. He testified that twenty-four members of his family were killed by the opposing tribe, but because of God's grace, he had forgiven them. What an incredible witness of the redemptive work of God!

My friend, Dave Butts, returned from Seoul, South Korea, following the Global Consultation on World Evangelism in 1995 to tell a story of two Rwandan believers, one a Hutu and the other a Tutsi, who had chosen to room together at the conference as a symbol of forgiveness within the Rwandan prayer delegation. Both had lost family members at the hands of one another's tribes, but their demonstration of great forgiveness impacted many hearts. These men showed that forgiveness and treating one another as they would like to be treated was more of a priority than the deep pain of their pasts.

According to Paul, Jesus has shown us how love is the fulfillment of the law: "Let no debt remain outstanding, except the continuing debt to love one another, for he who loves his fellowman has fulfilled the law. The commandments, 'Do not commit adultery,' 'Do not murder,' 'Do not steal,' 'Do not covet,' and whatever other commandment there may be, are summed up in this one rule: 'Love your neighbor as yourself.' Love does no harm to its neighbor. Therefore love is the fulfillment of the law" (Romans 13:8–10).

Connect with Christ

Prayerfully ask Jesus this question: "Lord, how am I doing with this command?" Allow the Holy Spirit to speak to your heart as you wait before Him with integrity and humility. Take some time (as long as you need) to quiet your spirit and wait before God. Allow this command to sink more deeply into your life.

Jesus, as I sit here in silence before You, please give me a more complete picture about what loving others as myself really means for my life. Speak to my heart so that I will know what You desire for me to do to embrace this command more completely and so that Your Holy Spirit can transform me more fully into Your image.

Consider the Command

1. How do you see that the Golden Rule is the fulfillment of the Old Testament teachings?
2. Have you known someone whose life was spent loving neighbors as well as he or she has loved him- or herself? How would you characterize his or her life in Jesus?
3. What do you need to do differently to more effectively love your neighbor as yourself?

Praying It into Practice

1. Thank the Lord that He treats you with grace and love rather than the way you deserve to be treated.
2. Ask the Lord to give you the supernatural ability to treat others in loving ways, treating them the way you would want others to treat you.
3. Who are you having the most trouble loving? Bring those people to the Lord regularly and ask Him to help you love them with His kind of love.

My Prayer

Father, I am so grateful for Your amazing love and grace toward me. Help me to learn from You and to love others as You love me. Pour Your love into my life that I might be able to treat others as I wish to be treated. Help me to take my attention off myself and put it onto You and the people you have made. May my life of grace-filled love reflect Your love to everyone I come into contact with so that Your kingdom can be lived out more fully in me.

Chapter 11

Fight Back by Giving

You have heard that it was said, "Eye for eye, and tooth for tooth." But I tell you, do not resist an evil person. If someone strikes you on the right cheek, turn to him the other also. And if anyone wants to sue you and take your tunic, let him have your cloak as well. If someone forces you to go one mile, go with him two miles. Give to the one who asks you, and do not turn away from the one who wants to borrow from you. (MATTHEW 5:38—42)

If someone slaps you on one cheek, offer the other cheek also. If someone demands your coat, offer your shirt also. Give to anyone who asks; and when things are taken away from you, don't try to get them back. Do to others as you would like them to do to you. (LUKE 6:29—31, NLT)

The parallel passages in Matthew 5 and Luke 6 share a difficult command for our human natures to absorb. We exist in an upside-down kingdom where sometimes the commands of Jesus seem not to make sense. His followers are to fight back when they are mistreated, not in anger or retaliation, but by giving kindness and forgiveness. All the way through these passages, Jesus is saying that Christians should give more than what can be taken by force. Revenge is a selfish, carnal reaction. Treating others as we would like to be treated, even though we are often mistreated, should be in the heart of every believer.

I dare say, as a whole, the church may be more disobedient in this area than in any other. Have you noticed how, for the most part, all the worldly alternatives of responding to ill treatment usually do not work well? Force only brings on more force in retaliation. Retribution escalates conflicts. Law courts usually end up costing more than if we had given as Jesus suggested. Maybe it is time we tried Jesus' way. You may say, "This command just isn't practical." Have you tried it? Forcible resistance doesn't work well. Often it only breeds more anger. Maybe we have forgotten an element: the divine dynamic. God can make it turn out better if we react according to Jesus' command, even though it doesn't seem reasonable. Romans 12:20–21 contains a quote from Proverbs 25:21–22: "On the contrary: 'If your enemy is hungry, feed him; if he is thirsty, give him something to drink. In doing this, you will heap burning coals on his head.' Do not be overcome by evil, but overcome evil with good."

If we are to follow this command, then we need to decide ahead of time that we are committed to obeying it. It is entirely contrary to human nature; therefore, we have to be filled with the divine nature. The Luke account says, "Do to others as you would like them to do to you" (v. 31).

We must be careful here. In the Matthew account, this is a

command without an accompanying promise. Jesus doesn't tell us how it will turn out. In fact, it may not turn out completely to our advantage every time. We are simply to trust Jesus enough that we will take this course of nonresistance just because He tells us to do so. Later in the passage in Luke 6:35, there is a powerful promise: "But love your enemies, do good to them, and lend to them without expecting to get anything back. Then your reward will be great, and you will be sons of the Most High, because he is kind to the ungrateful and wicked."

I found an extraordinary story about overcoming evil with good in R. Kent Hughes's book *Romans: Righteousness from Heaven,* volume 45:

> During the Revolutionary War there was a faithful preacher of the gospel by the name of Peter Miller. He lived near a fellow who hated him intensely for his Christian life and testimony. In fact, this man violently opposed him and ridiculed his followers. One day the unbeliever was found guilty of treason and sentenced to death. Hearing about this, Peter Miller set out on foot to intercede for the man's life before George Washington. The General listened to the minister's earnest plea, but told him he didn't feel he should pardon his friend. "My friend! He is not my friend," answered Miller. "In fact, he's my worst living enemy." "What?" said Washington. "You have walked 60 miles to save the life of your enemy? That, in my judgment, puts the matter in a different light. I will grant your request." With pardon in hand, Miller hastened to the place where his neighbor was to be

executed, and arrived just as the prisoner was walking to
the scaffold. When the traitor saw Miller, he exclaimed,
"Old Peter Miller has come to have his revenge by watch-
ing me hang!" But he was astonished as he watched the
minister step out of the crowd and produce the pardon
which spared his life." (p. 110)

The story doesn't say how Miller's enemy responded or if he
turned his life to Jesus, which emphasizes that likely our reward
for overcoming evil with good may come only in eternity. Yet, it is
always possible that by following the example of Jesus, who suffered
on the cross rather than inflict suffering, eternal reward will come
sooner than expected. Even so, a true disciple will obey Christ,
whatever the consequences.

Connect with Christ

Prayerfully ask Jesus this question: "Lord, how am I doing with this
command?" Allow the Holy Spirit to speak to your heart as you
wait before Him with integrity and humility. Take some time (as
long as you need) to quiet your spirit and wait before God. Allow
this command to sink more deeply into your life.

*Jesus, as I sit here in silence before You, please give me a more
complete picture about how to fight back by giving instead of through
revenge and anger. Speak to my heart so that I will know what You
desire for me to do to embrace this command more completely and so
that Your Holy Spirit can transform me more fully into Your image.*

Consider the Command

1. Do you agree with the author when he says that this command may generate more disobedience than any other? Why do you agree or disagree?
2. Have you experienced a specific time when you clearly obeyed this command? What was the result?
3. Do you believe the church needs more teaching in this area? Why or why not?

Praying It into Practice

1. Ask the Lord for the divine dynamic you will need to obey this command.
2. Pray for the wisdom to apply this command correctly to the situations in which you find yourself.

My Prayer

Lord, it takes a lot of faith to let You fight my battles for me. Give me that faith and help me to make up my mind ahead of time that I will not retaliate when I am wronged. Empower me through Your Spirit to respond to others as You would respond to them. Give me wisdom to know what is appropriate in each situation from Your perspective.

Chapter 12

Love Your Enemies and Pray for Them

You have heard that it was said, "Love your neighbor and hate your enemy." But I tell you: Love your enemies and pray for those who persecute you, that you may be sons of your Father in heaven. (MATTHEW 5:43–45)

But I tell you who hear me: Love your enemies, do good to those who hate you, bless those who curse you, pray for those who mistreat you. (LUKE 6:27–28)

But love your enemies, do good to them, and lend to them without expecting to get anything back. Then your reward will be great, and you will be sons of the Most High, because he is kind to the ungrateful and wicked. (LUKE 6:35)

In his commentary on this passage in Matthew, Adam Clarke says the principle in the three verses above is the "most sublime piece of morality ever given to man. . . . Who can obey it?" he asks. "None but he who has the mind of Christ. . . . Nothing but supreme eternal love can enable man to practice a precept so unsupportable to corrupt nature." The way to treat an enemy is to love him, even when he or she is unkind in word or deed. Extending this even further, Jesus not only commands us to love our enemies, but to *pray* for them!

Dr. Alvin VanderGriend, author and teacher, has developed an amazing strategy that embodies this command. It is called Prayer, Care, Share. When we begin to pray for someone, even an enemy, God moves in our hearts through the power of His Spirit to cause us to begin to care about and for this person. It is unavoidable. Prayer is God's love in action. Once we begin to care for the person for whom we are praying, we can extend acts of love and kindness to that person as opposed to avoiding them or treating them as they have treated us or others. As we show our love and care to them, their hearts may be transformed in such a dramatic way that everything about their lives changes. They may even become ready to hear the gospel if they have previously rejected it or have never considered the good news of Jesus. But, it all begins with prayer. When someone angers or frustrates you, begin to pray for them. Teach this to your children and grandchildren as well.

This command of Jesus has a promise attached. By behaving in a loving manner toward someone who has mistreated you, and by praying for the person, you will be considered a true child of your Father who is in heaven, for He is this way. "He causes his sun to rise on the evil and the good, and sends rain on the righteous and the unrighteous. If you love those who love you, what reward will you get? Are not even the tax collectors doing that?" (Matthew 5:45–46).

I don't know a better way to stop a fight than to stop fighting and start giving and loving. How many marriages would be saved if the partners could just crucify self and do what Jesus commands?

While visiting the Holy Land some years ago, I was struck by the strong emphasis on peacemaking in the Bethlehem Bible College. This school is led by one of the strongest Palestinian church leaders in the area. I recently learned the reason for his strong stand for peace in the midst of great conflict. In 1948, his father was killed by an Israeli sniper right in front of his home in East Jerusalem. His mother, left alone to raise seven children, urged them not to seek revenge but to obey Jesus' command to love their enemies. This has been lived out by this family to this day. The college leader's son, Sami Awad, is now the director of Holy Land Trust, a ministry that teaches nonviolence. His nephew, also named Sami Awad, spent a week in the museums of the Holocaust in Dachau, trying to understand what the Jews went through. Because of their obedience to the commands of Jesus, these two young men are highly respected by leaders on both sides of the Middle East conflict.

If you love those who love you, what reward have you? But when you love your enemies, and do good to them "your reward will be great" (Luke 6:35).

Connect with Christ

Prayerfully ask Jesus this question: "Lord, how am I doing with this command?" Allow the Holy Spirit to speak to your heart as you wait before Him with integrity and humility. Take some time (as long as you need) to quiet your spirit and wait before God. Allow this command to sink more deeply into your life.

Jesus, as I sit here in silence before You, please give me a more complete picture about how to love and pray for those who treat me unkindly. Speak to my heart so that I will know what You desire for me to do to embrace this command more completely and so that Your Holy Spirit can transform me more fully into Your image.

Consider the Command

1. How literally do you believe we should take Jesus' command to love our enemies?
2. What is a way you have demonstrated love for an enemy in your life?
3. Have you ever prayed for someone who has treated you badly? What was the result?
4. Is this a command just for individuals, or can it be brought into the life of a church or an entire nation? What would this look like? Can you think of any modern-day examples?

Praying It into Practice

1. Ask the Lord to pour His love into your heart so that you can love with His kind of love.
2. Ask the Lord to bring to mind those who might consider themselves your enemy, and then ask Him how you might demonstrate His love to them.
3. Ask the Father to give you His heart for your enemy so that you may see him or her as the Father sees that person.
4. Ask God to show you how to pray for those who are your enemies. Then put what you learn into practice!

My Prayer

Lord, it's true. This command is contrary to my natural human nature. Please so fill me with the divine nature that I can truly treat my enemies with the kind of love that gives. I ask You according to Your Word to pour Your love into my life. Show me those who might think of themselves as my enemy and show me how to love them with Your love.

Chapter 13

Open Your Eyes and Look

Do you not say, "Four months more and then the harvest"? I tell
you, open your eyes and look at the fields! They are ripe for harvest.
(JOHN 4:35)

Jesus had just told the Samaritan woman at the well that he indeed was the Messiah when the disciples returned from the city
where they had gone to buy food. The woman left the well and went
into the city to tell people about the remarkable man she had met at
the well. Meanwhile, the disciples wondered what Jesus could pos-
sibly have had to say to this woman, since Jews and Samaritans did
not associate with one another. (Read John 4:1–26 for context.)

When the disciples offered Jesus some of the food they had just
brought, He stated that His food was to do the will and work of
the One who sent Him; and, as if to prepare the disciples for what
was about to happen, He told them they should not always expect
a long wait between the time of sowing the seeds of life (as He had
just done in His conversation with the woman) and the harvest.

They should lift up their eyes and see the human beings around them who so needed the message He came to give. The needs were so urgent and the response of those hearing this life-giving message so immediate that the disciples may not always have to wait four months between planting and harvesting, as they did with some local crops. Jesus wanted His disciples to see that the fields were already ripe for harvest.

Indeed, many Samaritans, as a result of the woman's testimony, were eager to meet the One who had told her all she ever did, the One Who might actually be the long-awaited Messiah. They were "already ripe for harvest"—ready to believe. Jesus wanted His disciples to enjoy the fruit of the sowing He had done while they were off buying food, so they could rejoice together. He wanted to teach them to expect spiritual results even where they had not sown the seeds of His message. We never know how ready people are. Jesus calls us to be alert so that we can watch for hungry hearts.

In this particular command, Jesus is saying that we should always be ready to reap. Don't put off the harvesting. The gospel message is vital, life changing, and powerful. People lost in sin need the message now. Some will respond with faith instantaneously. As a wise evangelist once said, "You can be saved in an instant of faith." It doesn't need to take a long time.

This truth was convincingly impressed upon my mind when our quartet was singing in a revival meeting in a city in Kansas. We had been praying that God would allow us to help new people find Christ as Savior, as many had received Jesus at our meetings. We were invited one day to do a program on a secular radio station. While there, with fear and trembling, I engaged the radio announcer in conversation about Jesus. To my utter surprise I found that he not only did not resent my talking to him, but he was much more eager to talk about Jesus than I had been. He was "ripe for harvest." Although he did not accept Christ at that moment, I have to believe that God was at work in his life, and I was glad that I persevered through my fearfulness.

There is a wonderful promise in connection with this command: "Even now the reaper draws his wages, even now he harvests the crop for eternal life, so that the sower and the reaper may be glad together" (v. 36).

Connect with Christ

Prayerfully ask Jesus this question: "Lord, how am I doing with this command?" Allow the Holy Spirit to speak to your heart as you wait before Him with integrity and humility. Take some time (as long as you need) to quiet your spirit and wait before God. Allow this command to sink more deeply into your life.

Jesus, as I sit here in silence before You, please give me a more complete picture about how to open my eyes, look for people who are hungry to hear the good news, and be ready to share it with them. Speak to my heart so that I will know what You desire for me to do to embrace this command more completely and so that Your Holy Spirit can transform me more fully into Your image.

Consider the Command

1. It's an unusual command: "Open your eyes and look." Have you ever considered this a direct command of Jesus to you?

2. Have you ever been with someone who was "ripe for the harvest," someone who was absolutely ready to hear about Jesus? How did you respond?

3. How do you think you can practically bring this command for spiritual awareness into everyday life?

Praying It into Practice

1. Begin your day with a prayer, asking the Lord for open eyes to see those who are ready to hear the good news of Jesus and for the courage to share it!

2. Ask the Lord to allow these days to be days of great harvest for you, and for the body of Christ!

My Prayer

Lord, help me to share my love for Jesus with others, expecting that You can cause them to respond readily. Help me to be watchful for those whose hearts are ripe for harvest. Give me the courage I need to speak when I should and the wisdom to be quiet when I need to be. Thank You for allowing me to be a part of Your harvest work.

Chapter 14

Go and Learn What This Means

But go and learn what this means: "I desire mercy, not sacrifice." For I have not come to call the righteous, but sinners. (MATTHEW 9:13)

When Jesus came to Levi's home for dinner and sat with all of his friends, the Pharisees asked the disciples critically, "Why does your teacher eat with tax collectors and 'sinners'?" (Matthew 9:11). In reply, Jesus said, "It is not the healthy who need a doctor but the sick. But go and learn what this means: 'I desire mercy, not sacrifice.'"

Jesus was most likely quoting from Hosea 6:6, which states: "For I desire mercy, not sacrifice, and acknowledgment of God rather than burnt offerings." This same teaching is found in 1 Samuel 15:22: "But Samuel replied: 'Does the Lord delight in burnt offerings and sacrifices as much as in obeying the voice of the Lord? To obey is better than sacrifice, and to heed is better than the fat of rams.'"

In the same way that Jesus commanded the Pharisees, we are also to "go and learn what this means." Those who were criticizing Jesus were strict adherents to the old sacrificial system. They were criticizing Him because He was fellowshipping with the very people who needed mercy. His critics were overly concerned about observance of rigid religious rites, such as the rites of sacrifice, but they had little regard for the needs of those to whom Jesus and Levi were witnessing and revealing the mercy of God. It was not the old pharisaical system that would meet desperate spiritual needs of the people in Jesus' presence that night. It was the mercy revealed in the message of the gospel that Jesus and Levi were sharing. The Pharisees tended toward exclusivism. They kept to themselves and obviously feared polluting their fellowship by being in the company of "sinners." Jesus condemned that attitude and opened the door for the New Testament church to welcome and fellowship with those who need the gospel.

This concept was very important to Jesus, for He quoted this Scripture verse again in Matthew 12:7 when the disciples were criticized for picking ears of grain to satisfy their hunger as they went through the fields on the Sabbath. Jesus said that if those who were criticizing knew what this verse meant, they would not condemn the guiltless disciples. The gospel of mercy is much more important to Jesus than the strict religious observances of the Pharisees. It is more important to show love and to meet need than to fuss over religious rites.

We can think, "How terrible for the Pharisees to have such an exclusive attitude that they could not mingle with those who needed mercy!" But I believe that there are many in the church today who need to "go and learn what this means." We should think of this commandment when new people come into the church—new converts or even not-yet believers who are different from us. Some churches tend to reject outsiders just as the physical body tends to reject a transplanted organ. It takes a generous portion of the love of God and a comprehension of the mercy of God to counteract this rejection.

Mary was a prostitute and on methamphetamine. Her life got so messed up that social services took her daughter away from her. In her intense desire to get her daughter back, someone suggested she go to church. The person suggested a church near where she lived. She'd never been there, but the people coming out of the church seemed to be happy. One morning, going home from work with $800 in her pocket, Mary drove by that church and decided to go in. The pastor's message was "The God of Second Chances." Mary wanted a second chance so badly that she put the $800 into the offering basket and asked to see the pastor. It took the pastor awhile to figure out what Mary did for a living, but even so, he led her to Christ. That pastor showed mercy rather than judgment, and the congregation accepted, nurtured, and discipled her. Today, Mary is a pastor's wife.

Both the Old and New Testaments bear witness to the command of Christ to be merciful: Micah 6:8 states, "He has showed you, O man, what is good. And what does the LORD require of you? To act justly and to love mercy and to walk humbly with your God." James 2:12–13 says, "Speak and act as those who are going to be judged by the law that gives freedom, because judgment without mercy will be shown to anyone who has not been merciful. Mercy triumphs over judgment."

Connect with Christ

Prayerfully ask Jesus this question: "Lord, how am I doing with this command?" Allow the Holy Spirit to speak to your heart as you wait before Him with integrity and humility. Take some time (as long as you need) to quiet your spirit and wait before God. Allow this command to sink more deeply into your life.

Jesus, as I sit here in silence before You, please give me a more complete picture about what extending mercy to others rather than judgment really means for my life. Speak to my heart so that I will know what You desire for me to do to embrace this command more completely and so that Your Holy Spirit can transform me more fully into Your image.

Consider the Command

1. Do you believe the church often has the same problem as the Pharisees in missing mercy and following rules? Give examples.

2. How do you think you can obey the literal command "go and learn" regarding mercy?

3. Do you sometimes feel awkward when you are in a place that is predominantly filled with unbelievers rather than Christians? Why or why not? If you do have difficulty in these situations, how can you overcome that enough to share the love and mercy of Jesus?

Praying It into Practice

1. Ask the Lord to help you learn more of His desire for mercy in your life.

2. As you pray, thank the Lord for specific ways He has demonstrated mercy to you. Ask Him to help you pass that mercy along to others.

My Prayer

Heavenly Father, help me to understand that what is most important to You is mercy that results in salvation, not sacrifices and religious ritual. Show me the many ways You have demonstrated mercy in my life and then help me to pass that along to others. Forgive me, Lord, when I have gotten caught up in religious rules and activities and have judged people according to those things rather than Your grace. I thank You that Your mercy triumphs over judgment.

Chapter 15

Obey and Teach

*Do not think that I have come to abolish the Law or the Prophets;
I have not come to abolish them but to fulfill them. For truly I tell
you, until heaven and earth disappear, not the smallest letter, not
the least stroke of a pen, will by any means disappear from the
Law until everything is accomplished. Therefore anyone who sets
aside one of the least of these commands and teaches others ac-
cordingly will be called least in the kingdom of heaven, but whoever practices and teaches these commands will be called great in the
kingdom of heaven. For I tell you that unless your righteousness
surpasses that of the Pharisees and the teachers of the law, you
will certainly not enter the kingdom of heaven.* (MATTHEW 5:17—20)

The command here, though inferred, is what this book is all
about: Obey and teach the commandments. Do you want to
know how to become great where greatness really counts—in the
kingdom of heaven? Obey and teach the commandments.

Jesus was speaking to the multitudes seated on the mountain

near Capernaum. He said that opposing, breaking, or ignoring the commands makes one small in God's sight. But whoever obeys the commands and teaches others to obey them shall be called great in the kingdom of heaven. Jesus here was referring to the commandments of the law and the prophets as well as the principles He was teaching (Matthew 5:17).

When Jesus commissioned His disciples to go into all the world and preach the gospel, He added these words: "teaching them to obey everything I have commanded you. And surely I am with you always, to the very end of the age" (Matthew 28:20). We have given strong emphasis to evangelistic preaching of the gospel, but because the church has been lax on teaching the commandments, it is weaker and less effective than it should be.

When I was in South America to set up pastors conferences for World Vision, a Methodist bishop in Brazil said to me, "Our church is like a sack with two mouths. As fast as new people come in, others slip out." In Chile one pastor said, "Our church is spreading like prairie fire. It flares up quickly, but just as soon it dies out." Many pastors were not well trained and had no solid foundation for ministry. As a result of our conferences, pastors heard strong preaching from men like Richard Halverson, who later became chaplain of the Senate, as well as from strong leaders in their own nations. They experienced examples of good preaching and training on how to preach the Word convincingly. They also learned from teaching and practice the value of strong praying and obedience to the commands of Christ. Winning lost people to Jesus is vital, but "teaching them to obey" all He has commanded builds resilient, durable churches filled with kingdom-focused disciples.

These South American churches are not different from many in the rest of the world. Simply learning about how to disciple, however, is never enough. Good discipleship takes extreme commitment, time, effort, and much prayer on the part of church leaders. Then, the seed of the gospel must be planted in good soil and watered with the teaching of the Word, especially the teaching of the commandments and prayer. These things are not always easy to implement into the life of a church body. But when these things are firmly established, the church will grow and flourish.

Connect with Christ

Prayerfully ask Jesus this question: "Lord, how am I doing with this command?" Allow the Holy Spirit to speak to your heart as you wait before Him with integrity and humility. Take some time (as long as you need) to quiet your spirit and wait before God. Allow this command to sink more deeply into your life.

Jesus, as I sit here in silence before You, please give me a more complete picture about what obeying and teaching even the least of Your commands means for my life. Speak to my heart so that I will know what You desire for me to do to embrace this command more completely and so that Your Holy Spirit can transform me more fully into Your image.

Consider the Command

1. What commands do you think Jesus was talking about?
2. Have you had opportunities to teach the commands of Jesus to others? Would you feel comfortable doing this if you haven't had such opportunities? Why or why not?
3. Do you agree with the author that the church has focused

more on evangelism than on teaching obedience? If so, what do you believe has been the result?

Praying It into Practice

1. Ask the Lord to give you the strength of His Spirit not only to do His commands but to teach them to others.

2. Ask the Lord to give you a sensitivity in the Spirit to those whom you can teach the commands of Christ.

3. Read James 1:22–25: "Do not merely listen to the word, and so deceive yourselves. Do what it says. Anyone who listens to the word but does not do what it says is like a man who looks at his face in a mirror and, after looking at himself, goes away and immediately forgets what he looks like. But the man who looks intently into the perfect law that gives freedom, and continues to do this, not forgetting what he has heard, but doing it—he will be blessed in what he does." Ask God to help you always to be a doer of the Word and not just a hearer, so that your life might bring glory to His kingdom as you teach others.

My Prayer

Lord Jesus, I love Your commands. Help me not only to obey them, but to teach others to obey them. Lord, I know that I can only do this through the power of Your Holy Spirit at work within me. Bring into my life those who are ready and willing to be taught Your commands. Give me wisdom to teach Your commands with grace.

Chapter 16

Be Reconciled to Others

*Therefore, if you are offering your gift at the altar and there re-
member that your brother has something against you, leave your
gift there in front of the altar. First go and be reconciled to your
brother; then come and offer your gift.* (MATTHEW 5:23–24)

Jesus makes the above statement during a message on right relationships with others, especially with brothers and sisters in
Christ. It is no use to try to work out a right relationship with God
at the altar when one is living in a wrong relationship with others.

When preaching on this passage during a pastors conference,
one of the teachers said: "Nothing spiritual will happen until
there is reconciliation." Forget trying to offer a gift to God—even
the gift of your worship. "First be reconciled to your brother." It
is important to go to someone when you already know you have
wronged him or her, but it is also important when you aren't sure
or when the Spirit prompts you that there may be something you
are unaware of between you and another person. If you don't know

about a problem, God will not hold you responsible. But ask God to reveal the truth within your heart, and go to anyone you think might have something against you. It's a good idea to review our relationships with others each time we come into the presence of God in worship.

Years ago, I was a sailing instructor at a camp in Washington's Puget Sound. Sometimes the tide currents were stronger than the wind that was driving the sailboat. One time when the tide and waves were washing us into shore, I spoke too harshly to the one I was instructing. I hollered at him, to be honest. That night around the campfire, I could not get peace in my soul until I asked him to forgive me. I figured I had really blown it with him, regarding my Christian witness. Later one morning, he followed me out to where I was having a quiet time and we talked. The next morning we talked again, and he accepted Christ as his Savior.

It is always hard to say "I'm sorry," especially when one who is older has to go to one who is younger or when a father has to go to his child. But this is so important to God that Jesus said there is no use even trying to worship and honor Him until there is reconciliation. Keeping short accounts like this is about the only way to avoid resentments that can grow into bitterness, which can cause lives to be damaged.

I believe this commandment teaches an important requirement if we want to see revival in the church. Many of us have been praying for years for an outpouring of God's Spirit, but Jesus is telling us that we need to put feet to our prayers and be reconciled to one another before He will answer. A lack of reconciliation is what often keeps unity in the Body of Christ from occurring. It takes great humility to seek out a brother or sister and ask for or extend forgiveness. Yet, when we obey the command of Christ to do so, we open the heart of God to receive our worship.

Connect with Christ

Prayerfully ask Jesus this question: "Lord, how am I doing with this command?" Allow the Holy Spirit to speak to your heart as you wait before Him with integrity and humility. Take some time (as long as you need) to quiet your spirit and wait before God. Allow this command to sink more deeply into your life.

Jesus, as I sit here in silence before You, please show me what being in right relationship with others really means for my life. Speak to my heart so that I will know what You desire for me to do to embrace this command more completely and so that Your Holy Spirit can transform me more fully into Your image.

Consider the Command

1. Do you agree with the author that even worship will not be right until we are reconciled to others?
2. Do you know of someone whom you need to go to or communicate with in order to be reconciled with him or her? If so, what is preventing you from taking this healing step?
3. What do you believe would be the result in the church if we all began to take seriously this command of Christ?

Praying It into Practice

1. Thank the Lord for His reconciling work in your life through Jesus.
2. Ask the Lord if there is someone in your life with whom you need to seek reconciliation. Pay careful attention to

names that may come to mind as you pray this. Ask the Father to give you the courage to ask for or extend forgiveness to someone in order for a relationship to be made right again.

My Prayer

Heavenly Father, when I come to You in worship, speak to my heart if there is any relationship that needs healing. Even if I don't feel guilty, help me remember if someone has something against me and go with me to that person as we seek reconciliation. Lord, would You pour out that spirit of reconciliation upon Your people? Heal our relationships with one another as You have healed my relationship with You through Jesus.

Chapter 17

Let Your "Yes" Be "Yes" and Your "No" Be "No"

Again, you have heard that it was said to the people long ago, "Do not break your oath, but keep the oaths you have made to the Lord." But I tell you, Do not swear at all: either by heaven, for it is God's throne; or by the earth, for it is his footstool; or by Jerusalem, for it is the city of the Great King. And do not swear by your head, for you cannot make even one hair white or black. Simply let your "Yes" be "Yes," and your "No," "No"; anything beyond this comes from the evil one. (MATTHEW 5:33—37)

It is not good enough that we are careful never to swear falsely. Jesus commands His people not to swear at all, by heaven or earth, or by any person or place. Simply say yes or no. Jesus said, "Anything beyond this comes from the evil one" (v. 37). This is a significant teaching. It is the message behind the practice of Quakers and others who choose to follow it carefully. In such cases, most courts allow those with such conviction to say that they "affirm" rather than "swear" when taking an oath of office or testifying in court.

The bottom line of Jesus' teaching is that we are always to be honest. Because of their obedience to this command, the early Quakers gained a reputation for being trustworthy. Quakers do not swear oaths of any kind. In addition to the practice being clearly forbidden in Scripture, as we have seen, the act itself is illogical and to some extent, insulting. Quakers understand that when one speaks one is either telling the truth to the best of one's knowledge or telling a lie. The repeating of an oath does not magically change what is in someone's heart and implies that someone may for some reason tell the truth simply by virtue of taking the oath as opposed to simply being honest in all things.

To swear is to make a solemn appeal to almighty God as a witness to a statement or transaction, saying something such as, "God is my witness." In early times, the Jewish oath, "As the Lord liveth," was held sacred. Then, later, the rabbis taught that if God was not mentioned, then the oath was not binding. As a result perjury was rampant. Jesus was so against this practice He said anything more than a simple yes or no was evil. To say any more infers that you are so liable to be dishonest that there must be an oath before you can be trusted.

James 5:12 deals with this same theme and says that if you say more than yes or no you may fall under judgment: "Above all, my brothers, do not swear—not by heaven or by earth or by anything else. Let your "Yes" be yes, and your "No," no, or you will be condemned."

It almost seems that Jesus is saying, "Even if people won't believe you, don't drag God into it." God is not interested in verifying everything anyone says just because they mention His name. He is condemning people who treat oaths with contempt by making them casually or thoughtlessly.

In Craig Keener's commentary on Matthew (p. 192 ff.), the historical context of Jesus' statement is explained. Apparently, in ancient societies, oath taking was considered dangerous, since they essentially called upon a deity of some kind to execute vengeance in the event that the oath was not fulfilled. Therefore, a flippant or false oath was, in a very real sense, blasphemy because God's name was misused for wrong purposes.

According to Tekton, an education and apologetics ministry, "The Greek philosopher Pythagoras and others similarly taught, 'let one's word carry such conviction that one need not call deities to witness.' In the context of Jesus' own day, there existed a 'popular abuse' of oath-taking in which surrogate objects were introduced to swear by, so as not to profane the divine name—things like the right hand, Jerusalem, God's throne, and the head. Jesus also addresses this practice in his directive not to swear on such objects, as some thought it easier to break an oath if they swore on something inanimate rather than God." (See http://www.tektonics.org/lp/oathswear.html.)

People should know that they can count on what you say, and that no confirmation of any kind is necessary. We should develop such a good reputation for honesty that people will not require proof of what we affirm. We will be respected for such a stand. May God help us to guard our reputations.

Connect with Christ

Prayerfully ask Jesus this question: "Lord, how am I doing with this command?" Allow the Holy Spirit to speak to your heart as you

wait before Him with integrity and humility. Take some time (as long as you need) to quiet your spirit and wait before God. Allow this command to sink more deeply into your life.

Jesus, as I sit here in silence before You, please give me a more complete picture about what it means to be a completely truth-filled person, committed to making my "Yes" be yes and my "No" be no. Speak to my heart so that I will know what You desire for me to do to embrace this command more completely and so that Your Holy Spirit can transform me more fully into Your image.

Consider the Command

1. Is this a command that still stands today? Do you believe you can swear an oath in court and not break this command?

2. Is there an exception to this command? If the intent is just to speak honestly, is there harm in swearing an oath?

3. Do you have such a passion for honesty that people know they can trust whatever you say? If not, how can you set out to change that?

Praying It into Practice

1. Ask the Lord to give you a passion for always speaking truth.

2. Ask the Lord for wisdom regarding the taking of any oaths in the future.

My Prayer

God, give me a new understanding of Your position on swearing oaths. Help me to so speak and so live that those around me will know that they can rely on me to speak the truth. I thank You, Lord Jesus, that You Yourself are truth. As I speak truth, may it always be the truth in love that marks You and Your followers.

Chapter 18

Canceling the Debt

Peter came to Jesus and asked, "Lord, how many times shall I forgive my brother when he sins against me? "Up to seven times?" Jesus answered, "I tell you, not seven times, but seventy-seven times." (MATTHEW 18:21–22)

Here Jesus deals with one of the most important ingredients of the Christian system. I say important because after teaching the disciples the Lord's Prayer, Jesus explained, "For if you forgive men when they sin against you, your heavenly Father will also forgive you" (Matthew 6:14). So if we ever expect to see the inside of heaven we must forgive. Not just once or seven times, but without ever not forgiving. Seventy-seven times infers never-ending forgiveness.

To illustrate the importance of forgiving, Jesus followed this command with the story of a man who owed his master ten thousand talents. He begged for forgiveness, and his master canceled the debt. Then that man went to a man who owed him just one hundred talents and demanded payment. When that man begged for forgiveness, the man whose large debt had been forgiven refused and had him thrown in prison. When the master heard this, he turned the wicked servant over to the jailers till he paid the debt that could have been forgiven if that servant had not been so unforgiving. Jesus said that's how our heavenly Father will treat us if we don't forgive.

When I served with World Vision, I had a Chinese friend from Macao. He told me how he became a Christian. He was in business with a partner, and his partner stole from him, ruining the business. He was so bitter over it that his bitterness was eating him up. His former partner was getting along fine, but my friend was literally getting sick over his bitterness. He said he searched in his Buddhist belief system for an answer to his problem but found none. There was no provision in his religion for forgiveness. He learned, however, that Christianity had a forgiveness concept, so he converted, understood that God had forgiven him, and learned how to forgive his partner. Right away, he had peace.

Once, I wrote a sermon on this concept, which I titled "Forgive or Else." There is no alternative. In Hebrews 12:15, the Bible says if we don't conquer bitterness we will be troubled and many will be defiled.

So the benefits of obeying this command are wonderful. We enjoy God's forgiveness and all the rewards He has prepared for us. The consequences of not obeying this command are clear. Jesus gave the warning: If we don't forgive, God can't forgive us.

Connect with Christ

Prayerfully ask Jesus this question: "Lord, how am I doing with this command?" Allow the Holy Spirit to speak to your heart as you wait before Him with integrity and humility. Take some time (as long as you need) to quiet your spirit and wait before God. Allow this command to sink more deeply into your life.

Jesus, as I sit here in silence before You, please give me a more complete picture about what true forgiveness really means for my life. Speak to my heart so that I will know what You desire for me to do to embrace this command more completely and so that Your Holy Spirit can transform me more fully into Your image.

Consider the Command

1. Do you agree with the author that Jesus teaches unlimited forgiveness toward those who have wronged you? Why or why not?

2. Have you experienced the bitterness of unforgiveness in your life? How did you overcome that?

3. Do you believe that our salvation is dependent upon our forgiving others? Why?

Praying It into Practice

1. Give thanks for the Lord's forgiveness of your sin.

2. Ask the Spirit of God to search you and see if there is any unforgiveness that you are holding onto. If so, release that in prayer immediately.

Lord, help me to write to Max and ask his forgiveness and reimburse him for legal fees he had to pay related to Jet's Trust.

My Prayer

Lord, Your forgiveness is amazing. Your Word is filled with wonderful descriptions of how our sins have been forgiven, forgotten, blotted out, cast into the deepest parts of the sea, and removed as far as the east is from the west. Thank You! How can we help but live in that way toward others? Help me, Lord, to forgive as I have been forgiven.

Chapter 19

By This All Men Will Know

A new command I give you: Love one another. As I have loved you, so you must love one another. By this all men will know that you are my disciples, if you love one another. (JOHN 13:34–35)

This passage, along with the Great Commission, was part of Jesus' parting instructions to His followers. It was the essence of what He came to teach. It is similar to the second part of the greatest commandment—that we love our neighbor as ourselves. God is love, and His disciples are to be so known for their love for one another that this has been called the badge of Christians. People living outside the church see that love and they are drawn to Jesus. They want to get in on it. When we love, we let our light so shine before men that they see our good works and glorify our Father who is in heaven (Matthew 5:18).

Do you want to know how we are to love one another? Like Jesus loves us. Paul wrote, "Live a life of love, just as Christ loved us and gave himself up for us as a fragrant offering and sacrifice to God" (Ephesians 5:2). And in Colossians 3:12–14, he wrote, "Therefore, as God's chosen people, holy and dearly loved, clothe yourselves with compassion, kindness, humility, gentleness and patience. Bear with each other and forgive whatever grievances you may have against one another. Forgive as the Lord forgave you. And over all these virtues put on love, which binds them all together in perfect unity." There can be no greater love. I think the phrase "bear with one another" is important. When someone hurts us or offends, we are not to try to get even. We are to bear it in love. That's what Christ would do. And we are to forgive, as Christ has forgiven us.

There is a fellowship in the church that is like no other. We love to be together, for when we are together, Christ is in our midst. The fellowship is a precious experience, especially when we pray together, for Christ always lives to make intercession for us (see Hebrews 7:25). I feel He is right there among us praying with us and loving us. That fellowship, love, and acceptance is the promise that comes from following this command.

One of the members of our Four Flats Quartet (which became Barbershop Harmony Champions of the Pacific Northwest), became a student at our Christian college right out of World War II, not because he wanted to be a Christian, but because he wanted to be with a girl who was attending there. For a long time he resisted the Christian gospel. When we sang in churches and an altar call was given, he said his knuckles got white because he was hanging on so tightly to the seat in front of him. One day, during spiritual emphasis week, I gave him a list of all the reasons I thought he should give his heart to Christ and asked him to turn the paper over and list the reasons he should not accept Christ. He fumbled with the paper for a while, then he said, "I guess there aren't any."

That night he practically dove to the altar and gave his heart to Jesus and later became an effective preacher of the gospel. I believe that was a situation where we virtually loved him to Christ. He couldn't resist the love he saw in the believers on campus.

Connect with Christ

Prayerfully ask Jesus this question: "Lord, how am I doing with this command?" Allow the Holy Spirit to speak to your heart as you wait before Him with integrity and humility. Take some time (as long as you need) to quiet your spirit and wait before God. Allow this command to sink more deeply into your life.

Jesus, as I sit here in silence before You, please give me a more complete picture about what loving others really means for my life. Speak to my heart so that I will know what You desire for me to do to embrace this command more completely and so that Your Holy Spirit can transform me more fully into Your image.

Consider the Command

1. What do you think of the assertion that love is the badge of the Christian? If not love, what do you think would be our badge?
2. Do you think it is possible to love others as Christ loved us? Why or why not?
3. Is the fellowship in your congregation like the author presents? How can you best experience the love of Christ in your congregation?

Praying It into Practice

1. Ask the Lord to begin to pour His love into your life so

that you might love others as He does. (See Romans 5:5.)

2. Make a private list of five individuals within your fellow-ship that you have the most difficult time loving. Make them your special prayer project.

My Prayer

Lord, this command to love one another has to be so close to Your heart since it so closely reflects Your own nature and practice. Help me to love as You love. Pour Your love into my heart through Your Holy Spirit. Forgive me when I make excuses for not loving some-one. Break through hard hearts that have resisted Your love, even as they have proclaimed Your name. Lord, please make the congrega-tion I am a part of to become known as Your followers because of the depth of the love we have for one another.

Chapter 20

Making Disciples

Then Jesus came to them and said, "All authority in heaven and on earth has been given to me. Therefore go and make disciples of all nations, baptizing them in the name of the Father and of the Son and of the Holy Spirit, and teaching them to obey everything I have commanded you. And surely I am with you always, to the very end of the age." (MATTHEW 28:18–20)

This is the Great Commission, Jesus' last command to His disciples. Most Bible teachers feel that because He issued this command last, He meant it to have great importance for the church. Devout followers of Christ down through the ages have served tirelessly, often in the face of fierce opposition, to take the gospel message and make disciples in all nations, to all people groups.

While I was executive director of Evangelical Friends Mission, I was aware that the places where it is easy to take the gospel message had all been reached and now there remained places and cultures where Satan has had hundreds of years to put down his roots, and he does not give up that ground easily. We were also constantly monitoring our progress toward the fulfillment of this Great Commission, and I read and heard reports on the estimated number of people groups that still did not have a Christian witness among them. Because of the drive to fulfill this command, there is a strong emphasis on reaching the unreached—going to new people groups. Part of the motivation to reach all peoples comes from Jesus' words in Matthew 24:14: "And this gospel of the kingdom will be preached in the whole world as a testimony to all the nations, and then the end will come."

This commission is given in different forms in all four Gospels. In connection with the giving of this command in Luke 24:49, NKJV, Jesus gave another command, which I've chosen to include here, rather than to list it separately: "Behold, I send the Promise of My Father upon you; but tarry in the city of Jerusalem until you are endued with power from on high."

In Acts 1:8, He said, "But you will receive power when the Holy Spirit comes on you; and you shall be my witnesses in Jerusalem, and in all Judea and Samaria, and to the ends of the earth." Then the NKJV version says, "Now when He had spoken these things, while they watched, He was taken up, and a cloud received Him out of their sight." If we hope to be successful missionaries, then we must receive the Holy Spirit in all His fullness.

I'm convinced that the most successful Christian ministers have a strong emphasis on missions. C. W. Perry, the beloved pastor of one of the largest Friends churches, used to say, "The church God blesses gets outside itself." God honors a ministry that seeks diligently to fulfill this command. The wonderful promise in connection with this command is Jesus' promise to be with us always, even to the end of the age. All of us want His presence with us. I wonder if we can really have that if we are not in some way involved in the mission of seeking to take the gospel to all nations.

As an act of obedience to the second part of this command, I have given almost a lifetime to writing this book. (I started it while I was young, but I laid it aside for years when I was extra busy.) I saw that Jesus commanded us to teach others to observe all things He had commanded, but as far as I knew there was no book, outside of the Bible, that taught all the things He commanded. So it is my hope that this book will help us all to more effectively obey this important command.

Connect with Christ

Prayerfully ask Jesus this question: "Lord, how am I doing with this command?" Allow the Holy Spirit to speak to your heart as you wait before Him with integrity and humility. Take some time (as long as you need) to quiet your spirit and wait before God. Allow this command to sink more deeply into your life.

Jesus, as I sit here in silence before You, please give me a more complete picture about what going into all the world and teaching others to obey You really means for my life. Speak to my heart so that I will know what You desire for me to do to embrace this command more completely and so that Your Holy Spirit can transform me more fully into Your image.

Consider the Command

1. How are you obeying this command to go and make disciples?

2. The author wonders if it's possible to really experience the presence of Christ if we are not somehow involved in taking the gospel to the nations. Do you agree? Are you experiencing Christ's presence as reality? Why or why not?

3. Do you regularly pray for those who do not know Jesus? If not, what keeps you from doing so?

Praying It into Practice

1. Make a list of missionaries and missions organizations that you will commit to pray for regularly.

2. List those individuals that you know who don't know Jesus. Pray regularly for their salvation. Ask God for opportunities to be Jesus to them.

My Prayer

Lord Jesus, I want to follow You wherever You lead. You are so clear with Your command to go into all nations, making disciples, baptizing, and teaching. Please give me an increased passion for world missions. Show me how to pray daily for Your heart concerning the world. If there is any way that I am to be involved beyond my prayers and my giving, please show me. I want to move in Your authority to see You receive increased glory around the world.

Section Three

Personal: Inward Obedience

The inner life is often the most difficult of the three areas (God, Others, Personal) for us to control or change. We can be obedient in our love and worship of God (upward obedience), and focused upon loving and serving others (outward obedience) much more easily than we can submit to obeying Christ inwardly and allowing Him to transform our thoughts and motives day by day. It is easier to violate the commands that deal with our inner self, since it is easier to hide our disobedience. Lacking peer pressure to change, we easily become lazy and desensitized to our sin.

Yet, without obeying Jesus in our inner lives, anything else we do is merely deceiving ourselves and others. Confession, repentance, and the transformational work of the Holy Spirit in our inner lives are not things that a large portion of the church focuses on much these days. Perhaps if we did so, our lives would be more conformed to the image of the Son, Jesus Christ, rather than to the pattern of this world.

The purpose of obeying the personal commands given to us by Jesus is perhaps best reflected by Paul in *The Message* version of Romans 12:1–2: "So here's what I want you to do, God help-ing you: Take your everyday, ordinary life—your sleeping, eating, going-to-work, and walking-around life—and place it before God as an offering. Embracing what God does for you is the best thing you can do for him. Don't become so well-adjusted to your culture that you fit into it without even thinking. Instead, fix your atten-tion on God. You'll be changed from the inside out. Readily rec-ognize what he wants from you, and quickly respond to it. Unlike the culture around you, always dragging you down to its level of immaturity, God brings the best out of you, develops well-formed maturity in you."

As you pray through the commands in this section, consider how God wants to develop that "well-formed maturity" within you and yield to Him in obedience.

Chapter 21

The Kingdom Is Near

From that time on Jesus began to preach, "Repent, for the king-dom of heaven is near." (MATTHEW 4:17)

"The time has come," he said. "The kingdom of God is near. Re-pent and believe the good news." (MARK 1:15)

Some mark this proclamation to repent because the kingdom of heaven is near as the beginning of Jesus' public ministry. His ministry began when John the Baptist's public ministry ended—when John was arrested.

Jesus, hearing of John's arrest, withdrew into Galilee. He had been at His boyhood home, Nazareth. He moved to Capernaum, a large metropolitan city where He could contact the multitudes, in the region of Naphtali on the Sea of Galilee. This area had a larger Gentile popu-lation than did Judea. The people were living in darkness (see Matthew 4:16). They were more subject to pagan influence than were those in Judea. Because they needed Him most, Jesus went to them first.

He began his public preaching using the same text John the Baptist had used (see Matthew 3:2). He commanded the people to repent and believe the gospel, "for the kingdom of heaven is near." According to the prophet Isaiah, this kind of preaching brought great light: "The people walking in darkness have seen a great light; on those living in the land of the shadow of death a light has dawned" (Isaiah 9:2).

By this proclamation and this command, we can know that without repentance we will not enter the kingdom of God. Repentance is the gateway to the kingdom. Jesus said in Luke 13:3 and again in verse 5, "Unless you repent, you too will all perish." Entrance into the kingdom is the goal of repentance.

It is significant that Jesus started His ministry with this message. This is how Christian life and commitment must begin—with repentance. Virginia (not her real name) tried, or pretended, to be a Christian, but there was no power in her life, no fruit. I noticed that she spoke of her past life in sin almost boastfully. Clearly, no repentance had taken place in her life, indicating that she did not truly recognize her sinful condition before declaring that she was a believer. Unfortunately, because of this, she later returned to that life of sin. Perhaps what she didn't understand is that repentance is not about us. It is all about Jesus, who gives life.

In obedience to Him, our hearts become burdened to change and leave the intentionality and pleasure of our sin on the altar of a forgiving Father. We cannot straddle the world of sin and the world of righteousness at the same time, for they are mutually exclusive. Both worlds demand obedience that we cannot fully give without making a decision for one over the other.

We are not on believing ground until we have genuinely repented, turning from sin. Repentance is agreeing with God about our sin—godly sorrow for sin, being sorry enough to quit. In repentance, we come to the end of ourselves. We realize our own sinful conditions, and we understand we cannot save ourselves, but need a Savior. When this happens, and only when this happens, Jesus will save and usher the penitent into the kingdom of heaven. The kingdom is where God's will rules. This kingdom is upon each of us when Jesus becomes our King, when we turn around and become ruled by God, not by self. In the person and preaching of Jesus, this kingdom of heaven came near.

Some might think this kind of preaching would bring resentment, but it brought light and salvation. The warning here is clearly that without repentance there is no admission into the kingdom of heaven.

Connect with Christ

Prayerfully ask Jesus this question: "Lord, how am I doing with this command?" Allow the Holy Spirit to speak to your heart as you wait before Him with integrity and humility. Take some time (as long as you need) to quiet your spirit and wait before God. Allow this command to sink more deeply into your life.

Jesus, as I sit here in silence before You, please give me a more complete picture about what true repentance really means for my life. Speak to my heart so that I will know what You desire for me to do to embrace this command more completely and so that Your Holy Spirit can transform me more fully into Your image.

Consider the Command

1. We are not on believing ground until there is genuine

repentance. Do you agree or disagree?

2. Did the story of Virginia remind you of anyone you know? What would God have you do to help people like Virginia to decide who to serve?

3. Do you believe that repentance is a one-time occurrence or a way of life? Why?

4. Is the message of repentance good news or bad news for you?

Praying It into Practice

1. Thank the Lord for the gift of repentance. Ask Him to make you sensitive to the conviction of the Spirit regarding sin.

2. Pray that the message of repentance would be clearly preached from pulpits.

3. Ask God to show you whenever you need to lay down sin and ask for His forgiveness.

My Prayer

Dear Lord, I understand that without repentance there is no remission for sin. Show me if there is anything in my life for which I need to repent, and forgive me. Keep me so close to You and Your Word that I become sensitive to every sin and am able to move quickly into repentance.

Chapter 22

Launch Out into the Deep

When he had finished speaking, he said to Simon, "Put out into deep water, and let down the nets for a catch." (LUKE 5:4)

This command was given to Simon Peter. It took place by the Sea of Galilee. Jesus was pressed by the crowd, so to create a situation in which they could all see and hear Him, He got into Simon's boat, asking him to put out a little from the land. Then He sat down and talked to the people from the boat.

When he was through speaking, he said to Simon, "Launch out into the deep and let down your nets for a catch." Simon hesitated for a moment before he obeyed this command. Maybe he thought he knew more about fishing than did this strange man. Fishing was his business. "Master," he answered, "we've worked hard all night and haven't caught anything. But because you say so, I will let down the nets" (v. 5). Maybe the teaching Simon had just heard made him feel he should do what Jesus commanded. So they pushed out into the deep, and when they let down their nets, they had such a

huge catch of fish that the nets began to break. They beckoned to
their partners in another boat to come and help them. Verse 10 in
this same account says that James and John were their partners, and
came over to help. They filled both boats until they were about to
sink. Peter and all who were with him were astonished at the size
of the catch they had taken. The account says they forsook all and
followed Jesus. They had let Jesus use their boat, and He rewarded
them. But this was more than a thank you for the use of the boat;
it also contributed to their life support so they could now give their
lives to Jesus. When Simon Peter saw this, he was so convinced that
this man Jesus was extraordinary that he fell down before Him and
said, "Go away from me, Lord; I am a sinful man" (v. 8)!

While this command was given to a specific person in a certain
situation and is not to all people for all times, it has been quoted
many times to illustrate a truth that is often the theme of missionary conferences. There is much to be learned from the story of this
command. First, Jesus is interested in our temporal needs. He is
willing to give practical help. Second, it will be rewarding for us
to do what Jesus suggests even if we have tried before and failed—
even if it seems unreasonable to try one more time.

There were other instances when Jesus showed an uncanny
knowledge of fish. Remember when He sent Peter to find a coin
in the mouth of a fish so they could pay their taxes? (See Matthew
17:26–27.) After His resurrection, Jesus again stood by this same
sea and told His disciples to let their nets down on the right side
of the boat, and when they did they received a huge catch (John
21:4–7). Although Jesus became a man, He was obviously still God
and was all knowing. He would have been a great friend to take on
a fishing trip! In fact, He still is. I'm such a poor fisherman the only

Scripture I'm tempted to doubt is the one that says man shall have dominion over the fish of the sea.

Billy Graham had an experience like Peter's experience. He was coming to Los Angeles to conduct an evangelistic crusade in 1950. He had been through many evangelistic meetings before with varying degrees of success. As he and his friend and associate Grady Wilson were driving through the desert, Billy asked Grady to drive to the side of the road. There, for some period of time, Billy prayed. Jesus seemed to be saying to him, "Launch out into the deep." He could have argued that he had tried before and nothing special had happened. But in obedience, they went to Los Angeles, hired a big tent, and erected it in a major downtown district. The meeting went many weeks longer than planned, and God gave Billy such a large catch that the nets almost broke.

William Carey, the pioneer of the modern missionary movement, said, "Attempt great things for God and expect great things from God." Many leaders of great missionary advances have followed that advice.

The promise of this command is a large reward. The warning is that if we fail to obey Jesus, maybe because of past failures, we will miss the great reward.

Connect with Christ

Prayerfully ask Jesus this question: "Lord, how am I doing with this command?" Allow the Holy Spirit to speak to your heart as you wait before Him with integrity and humility. Take some time (as long as you need) to quiet your spirit and wait before God. Allow this command to sink more deeply into your life.

Jesus, as I sit here in silence before You, please give me a more complete picture about what launching out into the deep water really means for my life. Speak to my heart so that I will know what You desire for me to do to embrace this command more completely, and so that Your Holy Spirit can transform me more fully into Your image.

Consider the Command

1. Have you ever heard the Lord command you to launch out into a new area of life or ministry? How did you respond?
2. This is a command that brought real help to an individual. Have you experienced that response from God when you obeyed Him?
3. Have you ever had the experience where you have failed at something, perhaps even several times, and the Lord encouraged you to try one more time? What happened?

Praying It into Practice

1. Ask the Lord if there is some area that He is calling you to launch out into and let down your nets. Express your willingness to follow where He leads.
2. If there have been times in which you quit, or failed to launch into deep waters, confess that to the Lord, and ask Him to send you out again.

My Prayer

Lord Jesus, help me to stay alert for Your voice so I can obey when You tell me to launch out. I pray I will not miss the blessing You have for me by failing to obey. Give me the courage to launch into deep water when You are the One calling me there. Thank You for taking care of all my needs as I walk in obedience to Your Word.

Chapter 23

You Have Something to Offer

You are the light of the world. A city on a hill cannot be hidden.
Neither do people light a lamp and put it under a bowl. Instead
they put it on its stand, and it gives light to everyone in the
house. In the same way, let your light shine before men, that they
may see your good deeds and praise your Father in heaven.
(MATTHEW 5:14–16)

Jesus was speaking to the multitude on the mountain just after
he had selected His disciples. He was saying, "You have something to offer. Offer it! You are the salt of the earth" (v. 13).

Salt is absolutely essential. In 1968, during the Biafran crisis,
I was the director of the World Vision Relief Organization. We
wanted to get planes in to help the evangelical Christians, since
they were not being served by other flights bringing humanitarian aid to starving people. The flights were carried out at night
to avoid being detected by the Nigerian army, but even then,
our plane (I went on a couple of the flights) was shot at from the

ground. Administrators were hard pressed to make agonizing decisions about what they would carry on these planes. They could load just enough food to keep most of the suffering people alive. They hardly had room for gasoline for the trucks that delivered the food, but one thing they did carry was salt. Salt had high priority because it is a vital nutrient as well as a food preservative. By the way, while on a training flight, one of these crews hit a mountain and all lost their lives. Twenty-five humanitarian aid workers and pilots paid the ultimate price, trying desperately to feed the starving Biafran people during this horrible crisis. Yet, even in death, their light shone brightly.

We Christians are to hold a high view of our place in society when Christ is working in us. We are absolutely essential to the world around us. Salt is not effective when it is isolated or stored in one place. It becomes effective only when it is scattered. We are to scatter. Light is only effective when it is turned on so it penetrates the darkness. We are to be lights shining in dark places!

But what should be the result when people see our light? They are not to say, "My, what a pretty light." We are not lights so they will see how brilliant we are. In the light of our witness, they are to see the power and brilliance of our heavenly Father.

Jesus had just finished saying, "Blessed are the meek" (v. 5). A person can be meek and still understand his own value. It will do no good to love our neighbors as ourselves if we have no sense of our own God-given value. According to the meaning of the Greek word, a meek person is mild, gentle, kind, forbearing, and benevolent. But a meek person also understands well his own worth, as Jesus did. With proper self-esteem, we are to understand our importance and value as Christians, as the salt of the earth, so that we are able to let our light shine. At the same time, with proper meekness we are to be sure it is our Father in heaven who gets the glory.

Connect with Christ

Prayerfully ask Jesus this question: "Lord, how am I doing with this command?" Allow the Holy Spirit to speak to your heart as you wait before Him with integrity and humility. Take some time (as long as you need) to quiet your spirit and wait before God. Allow this command to sink more deeply into your life.

Jesus, as I sit here in silence before You, please give me a more complete picture about what offering my light to others really means for my life. Speak to my heart so that I will know what You desire for me to do to embrace this command more completely and so that Your Holy Spirit can transform me more fully into Your image.

Consider the Command

1. How do you resolve the tension between being meek and understanding your own value in Christ?
2. How well do you think the church is doing at being light and salt to the world?
3. Can you think of a specific example where Christ called you personally to shine your light in a dark place? What happened?

Praying It into Practice

1. Thank the Lord for being the light of the world and allowing His light to shine through you.
2. Ask the Lord to make you a "salty" Christian whose actions and presence create a thirst for God in those around you.

My Prayer

Heavenly Father, help me to be meek as Jesus was meek—mild, gentle, kind—and help me understand that I have value in Your kingdom. I want to let my light shine so that You get glory. Help your church not to hide our light but to take it to places of darkness.

Chapter 24

Turn from False Gods

If your right eye causes you to sin, gouge it out and throw it away.
It is better for you to lose one part of your body than for your
whole body to be thrown into hell. And if your right hand causes
you to sin, cut it off and throw it away. It is better for you to lose
one part of your body than for your whole body to go into hell.
(MATTHEW 5:29—30)

B ecause this strong statement was spoken by our Lord just as
He was dealing with the sin of adultery, we must conclude that
adultery, contrary to the views of the new morality, is a grievous sin.
We also know this command is important because the concept is
repeated in Matthew 18:8–9. Even so, this part of Jesus' Sermon on
the Mount has been troublesome to many. There is no record that
any of His disciples caused sinners to pluck out their eyes or cut off
their hands. But one thing is clear: We are not to make a moment's
truce with anything that might cause eternal death to the soul. If we
indulge the sin, it will gain strength and ultimately ruin us.

Adam Clarke, in his commentary on the passage, suggests this command refers to the idols or practices that perhaps have become too dear to us: "We must shut our senses against dangerous objects, to avoid the occasions of sin, and deprive ourselves of all that is most dear and profitable to us, in order to save our souls, when we find that these dear and profitable things, however innocent in themselves, cause us to sin against God." We hate to think of getting along without these idols.

This teaching could be applied to a friend or associate whose company or words causes us to sin. Cut this off quickly. Don't compromise. This is clearly the best way to handle an illicit relationship outside marriage. Whatever causes us to sin, no matter how dear, we are to separate from it, even by drastic means. If something keeps coming between us and God, keeps hindering us from obeying God, we are to cut it off. We must cast from us anything that causes us to sin.

The warning is that if we don't separate from the thing that causes us to sin, our whole being will be cast into hell. If we would be willing to endure an amputation in order to save the body, then how much more important is it that we take drastic means to save our soul?

In Thailand, the Sacred Fig is a fig tree species native to the area. It is believed to be the tree under which Buddha sat when he attained enlightenment. It is often thought that Buddha said, "To worship the tree is the same as to worship me." Animists believe that the Sacred Fig is inhabited by spirits and lost souls. Hindus believe that the deity, Lord Vishnu, was born under a Sacred Fig tree. The Thai people often decorate the trees with colored ribbons and sashes. "Spirit houses" and figurines are placed around the base of such Sacred Figs. Rather than chop the trees down, roads are built around them. The trees are a symbol of prosperity, good luck, and long life to many, and to damage one is to bring great dishonor or wrath upon one's person or family. How sad that so many people live in bondage to something created over and above the One who created it.

In my ministry overseas, where Satan has had his way for hundreds of years, when people respond to the message of the gospel and accept Christ, they often bring their idols and items used in heathen worship and burn them publicly as a testimony that they have turned from false gods to the True and Living God. This is true in our nation as well. For example, we have heard of entire youth groups burning offensive CDs, posters, video games, and so forth because they have been keeping them from a pure relationship with Jesus and tempting them to follow their worldly culture into sin.

Connect with Christ

Prayerfully ask Jesus this question: "Lord, how am I doing with this command?" Allow the Holy Spirit to speak to your heart as you wait before Him with integrity and humility. Take some time (as long as you need) to quiet your spirit and wait before God. Allow this command to sink more deeply into your life.

Jesus, as I sit here in silence before You, please give me a more complete picture about what turning away from false gods and sin really means for my life. Speak to my heart so that I will know what You desire for me to do to embrace this command more completely, and so that Your Holy Spirit can transform me more fully into Your image.

Consider the Command

1. Do you have a type of Sacred Fig tree in your life? What do you hold dearer than Christ? How can you deal with this?

2. When you first came to Christ, was there something you loved that you gave up for Him? We are not to make a moment's truce with anything that might cause eternal death to the soul. Do you agree with the author's statement? How do you deal with such things?

Praying It into Practice

1. Pray for spiritual discernment for things in your own life that might be an obstacle to greater intimacy with Christ.

2. Ask the Lord to help you take drastic measures if need be to put away any sin.

My Prayer

Lord, if I am in any relationship, habit, or practice that causes me to sin, help me to cut it off, even if it takes drastic means. I want to walk in purity and close intimacy with You. Help me to love You more than anything or anyone.

Chapter 25

Spiritual Nourishment

This, then, is how you should pray . . . (MATTHEW 6:9)

This is the phrase that introduced what we call the Lord's Prayer. Jesus had just been telling His disciples not to pray like the hypocrites and heathen pray, who think they will be heard if they use many words and vain repetitions. He told them how *not* to pray. Now, He turns to the positive. This is a good teaching technique. He was warning against being like the hypocrites. Now, He tells them what real praying is. And He gives us the model prayer.

One danger when we often recite something as familiar as the Lord's Prayer is that it begins to lose its meaning for us. Yet there is so much meaning in this prayer that we do well to examine it. The prayer has six or seven petitions, depending on whether you consider "hallowed be your name" a petition. The prayer starts, as our prayers should start, with an acknowledgment in verse 9 that God is our Father, and we honor Him. "Hallowed" means holy, consecrated, sacred, and revered.

What follows in verse 10 is perhaps the biggest petition we can pray: "Your kingdom come, your will be done, on earth as it is in heaven." This is what God wants us to pray, because the answer to that prayer is that all the earth and it inhabitants conform to His will. When Dick Halverson was leading the teaching team during the World Vision pastors conferences in Latin America, he referred to Ephesians 1:10 and said the kings and national leaders are not writing history, and the newspapers and commentators are not writing history. God is writing history, and all history is moving toward the time when all things will be put under Jesus' feet. On that day, this part of the Lord's Prayer will be answered. In fact, in smaller ways even before that great day, we can pray down the kingdom of God and the will of God in our situations now. And we should be doing that.

Next, in verse 11, Jesus reminds us that we should feel free to pray for daily provisions and that God cares about our daily needs. The prayer for daily bread may not seem big to you, but in many parts of the world among impoverished people it is an immense prayer. One of many documented stories told by and about George Mueller is this relevant story: "The children are dressed and ready for school. But there is no food for them to eat," the housemother of the orphanage informed Mueller. George asked her to take the 300 children into the dining room and have them sit at the tables. He thanked God for the food and waited. George knew God would provide food for the children as He always did.

Within minutes, a baker knocked on the door. "Mr. Mueller," he said, "last night I could not sleep. Somehow I knew that you would need bread this morning. I got up and baked three batches for you. I will bring it in."

Soon, there was another knock at the door. It was the milk-man. His cart had broken down in front of the orphanage. The milk would spoil by the time the wheel was fixed. He asked George if he could use some free milk.

George smiled as the milkman brought in ten large cans of milk. It was just enough for the 300 thirsty children. (See http://www.christianity.com/church/church-history/church-history-for-kids/george-mueller-orphanages-built-by-prayer-11634869.html.)

Directly after mentioning daily bread, Jesus added prayer for forgiveness in verse 12. Just as we need daily nourishment for our bodies, we need daily forgiveness to stay spiritually healthy. We should strive to live without consciously, willfully violating the known laws of God, but we need to pray this prayer to cover the things we know about and things we don't know about that hurt God or humankind. Note especially that we are to ask for and ex-pect the same kind of forgiveness from God that we give to those who sin against us. This concept is so important that it is the only one of the seven petitions that Jesus comments on at the end of the prayer. If we don't forgive others, we have no right to ask or expect God to forgive us, and if He does not forgive us there is no hope for eternal life.

Finally, there comes the prayer that God will help us to retain a right relationship with Him and avoid evil. We do this by staying away from temptation. Obviously, this petition will be answered only if we cooperate with God in the answer.

Many translations of the Lord's Prayer end by again giving glo-ry to God. He has the kingdom, the power, and the glory forever. It is as though the King has drawn a petition for us to present back to Him. Is there any doubt then that He will grant the requests? This is how we should pray. We do well to study this prayer and pray it with diligent thought and meaning every day.

Connect with Christ

Prayerfully ask Jesus this question: "Lord, how am I doing with this command?" Allow the Holy Spirit to speak to your heart as you wait before Him with integrity and humility. Take some time (as long as you need) to quiet your spirit and wait before God. Allow this command to sink more deeply into your life.

Jesus, as I sit here in silence before You, please give me a more complete picture about what the model prayer Jesus gave us really means for my life. Speak to my heart so that I will know what You desire for me to do to embrace this command more completely and so that Your Holy Spirit can transform me more fully into Your image.

Consider the Command

1. Have you ever used the Lord's Prayer as a model for everyday praying? How did that work?

2. What do you think about George Mueller's answered prayer? Have you ever experienced an answer like this? If so, describe it.

3. Do you agree with the author that perhaps our biggest petition is "Your kingdom come, Your will be done"? Why or why not?

4. Do you find it tempting just to gloss over the first statements of the Lord's Prayer in verse 9 as mere introduction? What do you suppose would happen if most of your prayer just focused on "our Father in heaven, hallowed be Your name"?

Praying It into Practice

1. Take the Lord's Prayer and divide it into three to seven segments or however many is comfortable for you. Each day, take just one of those segments, even if it's just a phrase, and meditate on it deeply as you pray it back to God.

2. Bring the request "Your kingdom come, Your will be done on earth as it is in heaven" into your own life. Ask the Lord what is happening in heaven that He wants to have happen right now in your life.

My Prayer

Lord Jesus, thank You for teaching us how to pray and for giving us this example of an effective prayer. May Your Spirit guide me to pray prayers that You are pleased to answer. Show me how to pray so that heavenly things show up on earth. Please continue to teach me to be a person of prayer.

Chapter 26

When You Fast

When you fast, do not look somber as the hypocrites do, for they disfigure their faces to show men they are fasting. I tell you the truth, they have received their reward in full. But when you fast, put oil on your head and wash your face, so that it will not be obvious to men that you are fasting, but only to your Father, who is unseen; and your Father, who sees what is done in secret, will reward you. (MATTHEW 6:16—18)

This is the third in a series of commands from Christ warning against the practices of the hypocrites. The first was concerning giving to the needy, the second about praying, and now fasting. There is a lot of similarity between these three practices.

In each one He tells us not to follow the practice that was primarily designed to draw attention to the worshipper rather than to the One we worship. In each, He shows that they have their reward—they are seen by men. Then He tells us how we should do it and concludes by showing that when we do it God's way, we will be rewarded by our heavenly Father, Who sees what we do in secret.

When we fast we are to do it quietly. It doesn't matter that others know you are fasting. It only matters that God knows. Have you been with those who seem to want everyone to know how religious they are? I know sometimes it's hard to conceal the fact that you are fasting when you are expected to eat with others. But to announce that you are fasting is not necessary or right.

The important point in this command is that Jesus indicates there is a place for fasting in the Christian life. He referred to this concept in another place when the disciples could not cast out the deaf and mute spirit. He said, "This kind does not go out except by prayer and fasting" (Matthew 17:21, NKJV). He endorsed fasting by His own time of fasting when He was led out into the wilderness by the Spirit to be tempted by the devil (see Matthew 4:1–2). His disciples understood that they also were to fast, for it was out of prayer and fasting that the first missionaries were commissioned: "While they were worshiping the Lord and fasting, the Holy Spirit said, 'Set apart for me Barnabas and Saul for the work to which I have called them'" (Acts 13:2).

Why should believers fast? Because fasting is turning from the physical to give emphasis to the spiritual. It is demonstrating to God that we want His answer to our prayer so much we are willing to deny physical appetite to get it. In a properly motivated fast, the very feelings of hunger become a part of the prayer we are lifting to the throne, so it seems to become more possible to "pray continually" (1 Thessalonians 5:17).

We know God doesn't want us to harm our bodies by any spiritual exercise. For this reason, few believers feel led to fast an unreasonable length of time, and I know some people with certain physi-

cal conditions dare not go long without food. But there can be very
helpful effects even physically from brief times of fasting, and there
can be very great benefits spiritually. *When* we do fast, however, we
are to do it for God, not to be seen by others.

I helped start Concerts of Prayer in Pasadena, California, in the
1980s. On the small committee that sponsored that movement was
a young zealous Christian named Lou Engle. He would quietly go
on extended fasts to seek the Lord, punctuating his commitment. I
could see early on that the Lord was going to use him in a significant way to advance His kingdom. Now, Lou has been one of the
main leaders in The Call, a movement of solemn assemblies focused
on prayer, fasting, repentance, and sacrificial worship. The Call
does not advertise the names of speakers or musicians (thus honor-
ing the command of Jesus to pray and fast without the intent of
being noticed by others); yet, thousands of mostly young people are
drawn to venues all over the nation to worship the King of kings in
deep humility of heart. God has honored the many years of Lou's
commitment to fast and pray in secret by drawing many into His
presence through these powerful solemn assemblies.

Connect with Christ

Prayerfully ask Jesus this question: "Lord, how am I doing with this
command?" Allow the Holy Spirit to speak to your heart as you
wait before Him with integrity and humility. Take some time (as
long as you need) to quiet your spirit and wait before God. Allow
this command to sink more deeply into your life.

*Jesus, as I sit here in silence before You, please give me a more
complete picture about what prayer, fasting, and giving in ways known
only to You really means for my life. Speak to my heart so that I will*

know what You desire for me to do to embrace this command more completely and so that Your Holy Spirit can transform me more fully into Your image.

Consider the Command

1. Have you ever fasted? What was the experience like for you?
2. Have you heard people say that fasting is an Old Testament practice and not necessary for Christians today? How would you respond to that?
3. What are some practical ways you can fast and keep it a secret from others?

Praying It into Practice

1. Ask the Lord about going on a fast. What would He want to do in and with you as a result of such a fast?
2. Ask the Lord to keep you safe from any temptation to appear spiritual in the eyes of others, whether through fasting, prayer, giving, or any other way.
3. If there is a medical reason why you shouldn't fast from food, ask God to show you something else you can fast from that will give spiritual benefits to your life. There are many good reasons to fast from television, video games, or frivolous activities, anything that keeps us from deeper intimacy with God.

My Prayer

Lord Jesus, help me to know when it is right for me to fast. Direct me in how I should fast and for how long. Help me do it for You, not to be seen as super-spiritual by others. I want to walk in humility before You and before others and not do things to draw attention to myself. Teach me how to develop a discipline of fasting with purity of heart and with the right motives, Lord.

Chapter 27

The Journey toward Perfection

Be perfect, therefore, as your heavenly Father is perfect.
(MATTHEW 5:48)

This statement to be perfect comes at the end of the section of Jesus' Sermon on the Mount when He was teaching about forgiving instead of retaliating and how to love one's enemies. Surely Jesus' admonition to be perfect has relevance to the verses just preceding it. One would have to be nearly perfect to keep the commandments Jesus has just spoken about. The Greek word for "perfect," *teleios*, means brought to completion, fully accomplished, fully developed, fully realized, thorough, complete, entire, perfect without shortcoming.

We are to be so filled with the love of God that we will be able to imitate His kindness and mercy even toward our enemies. God is to live in our hearts, fill us, and rule our responses so completely that there will be no place for anything contrary to God or inconsistent with love. We cry out that this is impossible! Nobody is perfect. This argument, however, reproves God who has given the commandment that we are saying is impossible to obey.

He calls us to live lives of perfect love, for in Jesus Christ, we have been enabled and made capable to do so. Because of Jesus, we can love as God loves. Our minds limit the word "perfect" and place it in a category that equates it with being totally sinless. Instead, we should look at the word as the process or journey of transformation every believer experiences who is obediently following the commands of Jesus. Let me suggest that what Jesus is saying in this command is: "You be as perfect as you can be, just as your Father in heaven is as perfect as He can be."

I was raised in a church that didn't teach much on the Holy Spirit, so when I got to college and heard sound teaching, I wanted all that Jesus died to provide. One night at the close of an evangelistic service when Dr. Lowell Roberts, who later became president of Friends University, Wichita, was preaching, I asked the Holy Spirit to come purify my heart.

In preparing my master's thesis, I was required to read one hundred books and study, in both Greek and English, the New Testament teaching on the ministry of the Holy Spirit. I discovered that while we can never be perfect in knowledge, in judgment, in our physical condition, and maybe a dozen other ways, it *is* possible, according to the Bible, to be perfect in two ways. First, we can have a pure heart. Peter, reporting to the Jerusalem Council (Acts 15:8–9) said that the Gentiles received the Holy Spirit as did the apostles on the day of Pentecost, "purifying their hearts by faith."

The second way it is possible to be perfect is described in 1

John 4:17: "In this way, love is made complete among us so that we will have confidence on the day of judgment, because in this world we are like him." We don't have to wait till we get to heaven to be perfected in love. When the Holy Spirit purges sin from our hearts and replaces it with love (Romans 5:5), we are then able to love God with all our heart, soul, mind, and strength. Understanding that God is not requiring some perfection that is not possible for me has given me a wonderful contentment in my desire to fulfill all the commands of Christ.

Through the death of His Son, God is able to draw us upward, to a higher standard than simply being a sinner saved by grace. We are so much more than that in the eyes of our loving Father. Because of Jesus, we now have the capacity and the commands to teach us how to set our sights on perfection, because it is His perfection rather than our own. We can only obey this command through Him and not in our own strength or by our own effort. There must be a difference between where we were before we came to Christ and where we are headed since! Yes, it is a high standard, but it is not instantaneous. Rather, it is our destination. You have likely heard it said, "The journey is the destination." As we follow Jesus, we will move closer and closer to perfection day by day. Our goal is to be like Jesus, who was without sin and completely followed the will of His Father.

God has given us the incredible grace gift to live higher and better than our sinful state. We have been given all the tools we need to take this journey, for we have been given new hearts, we are new creations, and the Holy Spirit has come to dwell within us and teach us all things.

Connect with Christ

Prayerfully ask Jesus this question: "Lord, how am I doing with this command?" Allow the Holy Spirit to speak to your heart as you wait before Him with integrity and humility. Take some time (as long as you need) to quiet your spirit and wait before God. Allow this command to sink more deeply into your life.

Jesus, as I sit here in silence before You, please give me a more complete picture about what being perfect as my Father is perfect really means for my life. Speak to my heart so that I will know what You desire for me to do to embrace this command more completely and so that Your Holy Spirit can transform me more fully into Your image.

Consider the Command

1. Have you ever struggled with this command of Jesus to be perfect? How have you chosen to deal with it?

2. "You be as perfect as you can be perfect just as your Father in heaven is as perfect as He can be." Does this statement help you deal with this command? Why or why not?

3. The author suggests that a pure heart and perfect love are the practical out-workings of the Spirit in our lives. Do you believe you can have a pure heart and perfect love? Why or why not?

Praying It into Practice

1. In prayer, accept the Lord's command to be perfect and ask Him to show you daily how that is to be lived out.

2. Pray specifically for the Lord to give you a pure heart and for His perfect love to be poured into your life.

My Prayer

Lord, I want to be as perfect as Jesus commanded us to be. Cleanse my heart by Your Holy Spirit so it will be pure, and fill me with Your perfect love. Please give me a greater longing to walk in holiness and purity. Help me not to make excuses, but to keep my eyes focused on You.

Chapter 28

Don't Worry, Seek God

And why do you worry about clothes? See how the lilies of the field grow. They do not labor or spin. Yet I tell you that not even Solomon in all his splendor was dressed like one of these. If that is how God clothes the grass of the field, which is here today and tomorrow is thrown into the fire, will he not much more clothe you, O you of little faith? So do not worry, saying, "What shall we eat?" or "What shall we drink?" or "What shall we wear?" For the pagans run after all these things, and your heavenly Father knows that you need them. But seek first his kingdom and his righteousness, and all these things will be given to you as well. Therefore do not worry about tomorrow, for tomorrow will worry about itself. Each day has enough trouble of its own.
(MATTHEW 6:28—34)

Clearly, in this passage our heavenly Father does not want us to worry. He repeats Himself twice, and in the midst of these commands, Jesus gives the antidote for worry; it is also a command, but one with a promise: "But seek first his kingdom and his righteousness, and all these things will be given to you as well" (v. 33). If we are not to worry, we must be an active part of the workings of the kingdom of God and we must be right with God in our thoughts, words, and actions. As we live out Christlike lives as followers of Jesus and as we align ourselves with His purposes and plans for His kingdom, He will provide all that we need.

Worry is epidemic even among those who are not poor and needy by the standards of the world. Yet, to cease our worry, Jesus says we are to seek His kingdom and His righteousness. First Peter 5:7 says, "Cast all your anxiety on him because he cares for you." We obey by giving our apprehension and concerns to the Father. He cares so much for us that He will carry these burdens.

Corrie ten Boom tells of the time when as a little girl she was worried about the future, worried that her father would die and leave her alone. Her father came to her bedroom and said, "Corrie, when we take a trip on the train, when do I give you your ticket?"

"Just before we get on the train," Corrie replied. Then he assured her that just as he supplied her need when she needed it, so her heavenly Father would supply what she needed when she needed it, but not necessarily before then.

I know a man who not only provides food for his own family, but also gets surplus, leftover food for many poor families in many churches. He told me he never asks for it. God sends it to him. He is definitely seeking first the kingdom of God and His righteousness. He is obeying the Lord. That's the secret.

How wonderful that God wants us to rest in Him. He wants to take care of our needs as we seek His righteousness. It is as if He is saying, "That's my job, not yours. It's too heavy for you. Let me handle it." Don't be anxious about tomorrow. Don't worry. Live like Jesus. Obey and trust God.

Connect with Christ

Prayerfully ask Jesus this question: "Lord, how am I doing with this command?" Allow the Holy Spirit to speak to your heart as you wait before Him with integrity and humility. Take some time (as long as you need) to quiet your spirit and wait before God. Allow this command to sink more deeply into your life.

Jesus, as I sit here in silence before You, please give me a more complete picture about what it means for my life to seek God and His righteousness instead of worrying. Speak to my heart so that I will know what You desire for me to do to embrace this command more completely and so that Your Holy Spirit can transform me more fully into Your image.

Consider the Command

1. Is worry a problem in your life? What sort of things do you worry about?
2. How do you understand the command to seek first the kingdom of God and His righteousness? What would have to change in your life to obey it more fully?
3. Can you remember a time when you felt God took care of your needs when you surrendered your worry to Him? If so, what was that like? If not, what do you imagine that would be like?

Praying It into Practice

1. Thank the Father for the astonishing ways He provides for

us. Tell Him how you trust Him for your provision.

2. Take time in prayer to obey the Scripture that says, "Cast all your anxiety on him because he cares for you" (1 Peter 5:7). As you pray, imagine yourself literally throwing any worries at the feet of the Lord.

3. Consider how you could be the answer to the prayer of another who is less fortunate than you are. Could you perhaps be the way God chooses to provide clothing or food for others to show them that they need not worry, for God knows what they need and has supplied it through you?

My Prayer

Lord, show me day by day how to seek Your kingdom in deeper ways and to continue learning how to walk in righteousness as Jesus did. Forgive me when I begin to worry and fret. Right now I come to You, casting my cares and anxieties upon you. Thank You for promising to take them from me. Help me to trust You more fully as I walk in obedience to this command.

Chapter 29

Persistent Prayer

Ask and it will be given to you; seek and you will find; knock and the door will be opened to you. (Matthew 7:7)

So I say to you: Ask and it will be given to you; seek and you will find; knock and the door will be opened to you. For everyone who asks receives; he who seeks finds; and to him who knocks, the door will be opened. (LUKE 11:9–10)

One of my prayer mentors was Armin Gesswein, who founded Revival Prayer Fellowship. He thought that ask, seek, and knock indicated degrees of intensity in prayer. First, we ask. Then, when we are in earnest, we begin to seek. Finally, when we are desperate for the Lord to answer, we knock persistently. This command is preceded in the Luke account with the story of the one who got help from a neighbor when he went knocking at midnight. He received because of his importunity (persistent asking). He just kept knocking, not stopping until his neighbor got up and gave him some bread to feed his hungry friend who had come visiting.

Seeking and knocking may imply that we are to do more than just ask. While we are asking, there may be things we can do by seeking and knocking to help bring the answer. Consider this interpretation of the passage: First, Jesus tells His followers to ask, making our needs and the burdens upon our hearts known to Him. Next, we are to look around (seek) with eyes of faith for how God might answer the things we have taken to Him in prayer. Following this, we knock expectantly by acting in faith upon the things that came to our attention as we were seeking God. Such active prayer persistence doesn't promote the idea that we are to sit around waiting for God to respond; it is stepping out in faith to seek how our heavenly Father, who wants to give good gifts to those who ask Him (see Matthew 7:11), will make a way for our prayers, offered in faith, to be answered in ways that bring honor to His name.

Jesus' teaching shows that God wants to answer our prayers as they are aligned with His will and purposes. He is more willing to give to us than we are willing to give good gifts to our children (Luke 11:13). He will not mock us. He, like an earthly father, will not give or withhold what would hurt us, but He longs to reward our faith.

In a church I pastored, I knew a woman who for years kept on asking God to save her husband. She wouldn't give up, but kept on praying. He had heart trouble and nearly died, but God spared him in answer to her prayers and the prayers of others in the church. He lived just a few more years, but during that time he gave his heart to Jesus and his life was gloriously changed. What might have happened had she given up and not persisted? It's very likely that her precious husband may never have entered into relationship with Jesus.

The Bible says God knows what we need before we ask, but He waits for us to ask. He has ordained that we get what we need from Him by asking, seeking, and knocking. There are times when His timetable is different than ours. Sometimes He waits until there is no way the answer can come without the glory going to Him. But He longs to answer our prayers, because He loves to respond to His children's requests.

To you who feel you have asked and not received, let me remind you that Scripture teaches that we must ask according to the will of God (1 John 5:14–15). This is why it is so important to be filled with knowledge of the Word of God, so we know what God loves to give. My wife and I heard a preacher in a series of meetings who led us to write down the prayer requests that were important to us but were also ones that we felt were in accordance to the will of God. We were to pray them daily until we saw God answer. We decided to give it a try and were amazed as God answered every one of them. That was a great encouragement to our faith. It's right to take God at His Word.

This is a command with a glorious promise. As you are persistent in prayer that has been aligned with the will of the Father, you will receive from Him as you ask, you will find as you seek, and the door will be opened for you as you knock. Take time to look around you to see what God is doing and what He may be showing you in the process. He longs to interact with you in the context of His kingdom on earth as you engage heaven.

Connect with Christ

Prayerfully ask Jesus this question: "Lord, how am I doing with this command?" Allow the Holy Spirit to speak to your heart as you

wait before Him with integrity and humility. Take some time (as long as you need) to quiet your spirit and wait before God. Allow this command to sink more deeply into your life.

Jesus, as I sit here in silence before You, please give me a more complete picture about what being persistent in prayer really means for my life. Speak to my heart so that I will know what You desire for me to do to embrace this command more completely and so that Your Holy Spirit can transform me more fully into Your image.

Consider the Command

1. What do you think of the idea that asking, seeking, and knocking describe increasing intensity in prayer? Is that a helpful concept to you?

2. In light of Jesus' promises regarding prayer, how do you personally handle prayers that appear to go unanswered?

3. Do you believe the author's assertion that God longs to answer our prayers? How does or will this truth impact the way you pray?

Praying It into Practice

1. Thank the Father for initiating prayer and for promising to answer our prayers as we pray what is on His heart and in His will.

2. Ask the Lord to take you deeper in understanding prayer, showing you what it means to progress from asking, to seeking, to knocking.

3. As you spend time in God's Word, practice praying about things you discover that are clearly upon His heart.

My Prayer

Father, I am in awe of the fact that You hear and answer my prayers. I thank You that prayer is even more important to You than it is to me. Would You make me a person of prayer? Show me how to ask and seek and knock in a way that lines up with Your purposes. Teach me to pray so that Your power is released, Your will is accomplished, and so that You receive honor and glory.

Chapter 30

Narrow Gate

*Make every effort to enter through the narrow door, because
many, I tell you, will try to enter and will not be able to.*
(LUKE 13:24)

J esus was going through cities and villages, teaching with His
disciples when someone asked him, "Lord, are only a few people
going to be saved?" (Luke 13:22). That's when Jesus spoke the
words of this command about entering through the narrow door.
Then He painted the picture of the Master of the house closing the
door, as people stand outside and knock, pleading to be admitted
based on the fact that they ate and drank in His presence. And the
Master will say, "I don't know you or where you come from. . . .
Away from me, all you evildoers! There will be weeping there, and
gnashing of teeth" (v. 26–28).

Basically, Jesus is stating that many "good" people assume they
are going to heaven even though they have never submitted to the
Lordship of Jesus and never dealt with the issue of sin in their lives.

Romans 6:23 tells us that the wages of sin is death. And the solution to that problem is that Jesus died in our place, taking on Himself the penalty of sin for all who will repent of their sin, ask Him for forgiveness, and trust Him as their Lord and Savior.

The people who don't make it into heaven are those who trust in something else as the ticket for admittance, such as good works or some false religion. They have not, however, spent their lives in pursuit of becoming like Christ. Others subscribe to the worldview that there are many ways to God although there is only one: "Jesus answered, 'I am the way and the truth and the life. No one comes to the Father except through me'" (John 14:6).

In Bible times when sheepherders could not make it back to the fold at night, they would make a ring with rocks and bring the sheep inside that ring. Then the shepherd himself would lie down at the opening to protect the sheep from predators. He would act as the door, the narrow gate.

I was once in a meeting in London with some church workers who considered their own ideas and feelings as at least as authoritative as the Scriptures. We were talking about John 14:6. And one said, "Oh, I wouldn't teach that. That is so exclusive and arrogant." My friend Keith Sarver, a fellow evangelical, said, "I didn't say it. Jesus did."

Yes, it is a narrow gate and few there be that find it, but it is the gate God has established. "For God so loved the world that he gave his one and only Son, that whoever believes in him shall not perish but have eternal life" (John 3:16). If there were any other way to heaven, do you think God would have paid so great a price?

Connect with Christ

Prayerfully ask Jesus this question: "Lord, how am I doing with this command?" Allow the Holy Spirit to speak to your heart as you wait before Him with integrity and humility. Take some time (as long as you need) to quiet your spirit and wait before God. Allow this command to sink more deeply into your life.

Jesus, as I sit here in silence before You, please give me a more complete picture about what entering through the narrow gate really means for my life. Speak to my heart so that I will know what You desire for me to do to embrace this command more completely and so that Your Holy Spirit can transform me more fully into Your image.

Consider the Command

1. Do you believe that Jesus is the only way to salvation? Why or why not?

2. Why do you think so many people do not deal with sin in their lives? Is it difficult for you? Why or why not?

3. How do you answer those who say that passages like this are too exclusive and intolerant of other beliefs?

4. How does the sacrifice Jesus made on the cross so that you could live forever in heaven affect you when you consider it? Compare this to the shepherd making a ring around his sheep and then lying down at the entrance to guard them.

Praying It into Practice

1. Thank the Lord for being our door, our place of entry into the kingdom of God. Worship Him as the Way, the Truth, the Life!

2. Pray for those whom you know who do not yet know that Jesus is the Narrow Way, who have not yet accepted Him as their Savior and Lord.

My Prayer

Lord, I am overwhelmed by Your grace and love that has brought me into Your kingdom, not by my works but through Your very person. You are the Narrow Gate! Help me to stay in the Way that is You. I pray for my family and friends who do not yet know You and who have not yet entered through the Narrow Gate. Please lead them to Yourself, heavenly Shepherd.

Keep Praying

We trust this book was a meaningful experience for you in encountering Jesus. If you would like to continue praying the commands of Christ into your life, you can find additional ones in a downloadable document at:

www.havestprayer.com/resources/free-downloads
